DONALD S. LUTZ

MW01027605

The Origins *of* American Constitutionalism

Louisiana State University Press
Baton Rouge and London

97   96   95   94   93   92   91   90   89   88   5   4   3   2   1

Designer: Laura Roubique Gleason
Typeface: Primer
Typesetter: The Composing Room of Michigan, Inc.
Printer: Thomson-Shore, Inc.
Binder: John H. Dekker & Sons, Inc.

Library of Congress Cataloging-in-Publication Data
Lutz, Donald S.
    The origins of American constitutionalism / Donald S. Lutz.
      p. cm.
    Includes index.
    ISBN 0-8071-1479-0 (alk. paper).   ISBN 0-8071-1506-1 (pbk. : alk.
paper)
      1. United States—Constitutional history.   I. Title.
KF4541.L87 1988
342.73′029—dc19
[347.30229]   88-6415
                                      CIP

Published with the assistance of a grant from the New York State Commission on the
Bicentennial of the United States Constitution.

Parts of Chapter 11 were originally published as "The Relative Influence of European
Writers on Late Eighteenth-Century American Political Thought," in *American
Political Science Review*, LXXVIII (1984), 189–97.

The paper in this book meets the guidelines for permanence and durability of the
Committee on Production Guidelines for Book Longevity of the Council on Library
Resources. ∞

For Linda and Austin

Contents

Acknowledgments

Every author incurs debts while writing a book. The Introduction describes most of the intellectual debts I owe, but special mention must be made of Daniel J. Elazar. After I had discovered for myself how important covenant ideas were for American political thought, he included me in a series of Covenant Workshops at the Center for the Study of Federalism. My discussions with him and more than one hundred scholars from around the world constituted almost a second education. This book bears the positive marks of many talks with Elazar and with Ellis Katz, John Kincaid, Stephen Schechter, Vincent Ostrom, and others too numerous to mention. To these men I wish to express my sincere thanks.

I would also like to thank two private foundations for their support. Liberty Fund, through its seminars and colloquiums, provided an opportunity for discussing with scholars from my own and other disciplines several of the texts and authors used here—ranging from Locke, Montesquieu, and Hume to the Fundamental Orders of Connecticut. Liberty Fund, and the scholars I have met through its auspices, have significantly contributed to this book. The Earhart Foundation, of Ann Arbor, Michigan, provided generous support for a leave of absence from teaching during which much of the manuscript was written. Despite support from these various sources, the author bears sole responsibility for any errors.

The Origins *of* American Constitutionalism

Introduction: The Nature of the Task

If there is a Muse for what follows, it is not Clio but Aristotle. Rather than a history, this work in political theory focuses upon constitutions. My aim is to recover and analyze the basis for the American constitutional tradition. Hence, the title reflects an interest not only in the origin of the United States Constitution but in the constitutional tradition of which it is a part.

American political theory is fundamentally grounded in the notion of constitutionalism, and the United States is above all a constitutional political order. Even more, the American people, building upon their British heritage and their own experience, invented modern constitutionalism and bequeathed it to the world. The importance of this contribution can be easily summarized. In 1787 the only written constitutions in the world existed in English-speaking America; today, almost every nation feels it necessary to have such a document. Even though most nations do not have true constitutional government despite their having constitutions, those living under a constitutional government number almost one billion people, and another billion and a half live in countries struggling to achieve constitutionalism.

America has also exported many specific principles of constitutional design. For example, federalism has been widely adopted and adapted, and is an extremely important "technological transfer." Americans have not made any money on such transfers, at least in a direct sense, but try to imagine the costs we would have to bear if ours were the only constitutional order. Not only would our own rights be less secure, but protecting our way of life in such a world would be considerably more expensive. Nor would economic exchanges with other nations have led to the material prosperity we now enjoy. Ultimately, constitutionalism may be the most important, the most cost-effective, the most historically crucial invention for the American way of life ever to emerge from this country. The United States Patent Office may be forgiven for ignoring constitutionalism, but those writing on American politics cannot.

Twenty-five years ago, George W. Carey first led me to engage in close textual analysis of the United States Constitution. Five years later, Charles S. Hyneman led me to engage again in that close textual analysis, this time with the admonition to determine whether the text was complete. At this point I discovered something that writers on American political theory had failed to tell me: there were thirteen state constitutions in existence in 1787, and they were part of the national document. Referred to directly or by implication more than fifty times in forty-two sections of the U.S. Constitution, these state constitutions had to be read in order to understand what the document said.

Unprepared for what I found in these documents, and limited largely to Allan Nevins' 1924 analysis, which was often hostile to their contents, I set out to recover from the original documents the contribution of the early state constitutions to the American Constitution. A few years into the process Gordon Wood published his seminal *The Creation of the American Republic*. My first book, *Popular Consent and Popular Control* (1980), was influenced by the work of this eminent historian, though I was more interested in coherent Whig political theory than in history.

In that research I came across a rich vein that had been only slightly tapped, notably by Bernard Bailyn—the pamphlets and newspaper articles of the founding era. Unaware of Herbert Storing's roughly parallel work in progress, I joined forces with Charles Hyneman to publish some of the best of this political literature along with an extensive bibliography of much that could not be reproduced in *American Political Writing During the Founding Era* (1983). Research on the state constitutions also led me to examine their origins, and I went back through the colonial documents of political foundation to the early seventeenth century. I had previously only dimly perceived the existence of such documents, and what I found was not only a world almost totally ignored by political scientists but also the essential origins of American constitutionalism.

I relied on Andrew C. McLaughlin's *Foundations of American Constitutionalism* (1932), an excellent work all but forgotten by historians and political scientists alike. Using entirely different methods, I ended up supporting many of McLaughlin's general conclusions. As influential on my study of colonial and early national documents was the work of Daniel J. Elazar, especially his recovery of the relevance of covenant theory for Western and American political theory. In the shadow of these two men, I published articles detailing the colonial and early statehood background to American constitutionalism. Because the colonial documents were themselves so inaccessible and so little appreciated, I published a collection along with an initial analysis in *Documents of Political Foundation Written by Colonial Americans* (1986). The large task remained of treating comprehensively all that I had found during these two decades of research. That is the purpose of the present volume.

Historians, beginning with Pocock, Bailyn, and Wood, have done a superb job of recovering the historical basis for early American political thought. This rich resurgence of historical scholarship follows, with only a few notable exceptions, almost half a century of neglecting the founding era. Political theorists were slow to catch on, perhaps because so few in political science read history anymore. With the advent of the Bicentennial, many were led to look up from close textual analysis of isolated texts and take the example of some of their more advanced brethren, among them Martin Diamond, Herbert Storing, Charles Hyneman, George Carey, and Willmoore Kendall. They began the process of carefully, comprehensively recovering the grounds of American political theory as theory.

The U.S. Constitution stands at the apex of American tradition, but it remains simply another political document unless we choose to use it in a certain way, as the summary of our political commitments and as the standard by which we assess, develop, and run our political system. To use a constitution in this way is the essence of constitutionalism.

A constitution provides a definition for a way of life. It contains the essential political commitments of a people and is a collective, public expression of particular importance. One can read a letter to gain insight into the mind of an individual, or read a set of treatises and pamphlets to obtain a sense of the range of positions on a particular issue. A constitution, a document of political founding or refounding, however, amounts to a comprehensive picture of a people at a given time.

Reading properly and carefully, one can glean from a constitution the balance of political forces, a structure for preserving or enhancing that balance, a statement of the way people should treat each other, and the values that form the basis for the people's working relationship, as well as the serious, remaining problems in the political order. Those problems become evident in the "seams," the points at which the Framers are straining to paper over or finesse internal contradictions, such as the presence of slavery in a system committed to individual liberty. Moreover, constitutions should be taken seriously as architectonic plans. The idea of constitutionalism itself requires that.

The discussion will at times resemble a history in that I will take documents and events in chronological order and connect earlier documents and later ones. The phenomenon under study dictates the diachronic approach. Eric Voegelin, another Muse, says that foundation documents evolve over time and tend to elaborate upon what is contained embryonically in earlier documents. This is indeed the case in America, and so that approach is necessary. The progression, however, is not inevitable. The process could at any time have been derailed, terminated, or moved in a different direction.

The discussion will also make use of history, summarizing the findings of many historians. The meanings of words and categories of thought shift, and one must be careful not to commit an anachronism. There are continuing controversies among historians, especially as regards the founding, but talking about them is not necessarily participating in the debate. Attempts here to show how evidence in the foundation documents does or does not support historical analysis are intended primarily to reveal the meaning of the texts.

Probably the best recent historical work on the Constitution is Forrest McDonald's *Novus Ordo Seclorum* (1985). A brief comparison with that work will serve to set off my approach. Although the subtitle speaks of the origins of the Constitution, McDonald early makes clear his interest in the sources of ideas used in the Constitution rather than its origins as a document in itself, or in the origins of American constitutionalism generally. Also, he is interested more in the intellectual history of those ideas than in their political manifestation. Thus, for example, since constitutions are not intellectual treatises, he looks to the writings of European thinkers rather than to the earlier American documents of political foundation.

The point here is not to criticize the one book written by a historian that all political scientists should read. In this study I examine the ideas found in political documents by looking first at the political documents and then at the writings of political theorists. McDonald, in explicating the Constitution, does not discuss those parts that produce the extended republic, which James Madison found so central to the architectonic plan of the document. I, however, give close attention to such passages. The United States Constitution never mentions federalism, the extended republic, virtue, legislative supremacy, checks and balances, separation of powers, mixed regime, or rights, but they are all there. I am interested primarily in political institutions and their theoretical basis, and only secondarily in their ideological justification.

Finally, the root word for history, *histeme,* means storytelling. Perhaps in this sense what follows is a history, my recounting how groups of peoples founded and refounded themselves to create modern constitutionalism, and then re-founded themselves as a nation to create a federal republican constitution. But my hope is that my focus upon the public documents, especially those consensual documents of political foundation, will allow the people themselves to tell the story in their own words in the only writing designed specifically and consciously to speak for them all together. The appropriate Muses having been invoked, it is time to begin the story.

1. The Problem of Origins

Americans are the heirs of a constitutional tradition that was mature by the time of the national Constitution. Derived in part from English constitutional theory and practice, American constitutionalism is nevertheless distinct from that tradition. In accounting for the differences, we must come to terms with the origins of the American variant.

Until 1776, Americans were British subjects living under a constitutional monarchy. From the first British settlement in North America until the break with Britain should have been time enough to make them thoroughly British in their political inclinations. The longer they lived along the eastern seaboard, however, the less did they resemble their peers in the mother country when it came to the fundamental design of political institutions. With independence, Americans did not so much reject the British constitution as affirm their own constitutional tradition. They tested that tradition between 1776 and 1787 by writing two dozen state constitutions and the national Articles of Confederation. Then, in the summer of 1787, Americans brought to completion the tradition of constitutional design they had begun more than a century and a half earlier.

Because it represents a kind of historical culmination, or perhaps the critical historical synthesis, the United States Constitution is the logical place to begin. Certainly we will be much interested in its form, content, and theoretical underpinnings. At the same time, even a quick reading of the document shows that the states are mentioned ubiquitously. We cannot understand much of what we find in the national document without also reading the state constitutions in effect at that time. It would not be putting the matter too strongly to say that the United States Constitution, as a *complete* foundation document, includes the state constitutions as well. This fundamental aspect of the American political tradition is part of what must be accounted for, and it has no precursor in the British tradition.

The situation becomes immediately more problematic when we remember that three of the operational state constitutions in 1789 were slightly modified charters dating from the 1600s. The people of Rhode Island, Massachusetts, and Connecticut found no reason to change their government at all when they became independent. It seems that many Americans viewed themselves as essentially self-governing long before the break with Britain, and even prior to wanting independence.

Where are we to begin, then, if not in 1789? Eric Voegelin suggests that political analysis should start with a people's attempt at self-definition or self-interpretation, and this is most likely to be found in their political documents and political writing.[1] At some point, if a political system is to endure, a people must constitute themselves *as a people* by achieving a shared psychological state in which they recognize themselves as engaged in a common enterprise and as bound together by widely held values, interests, and goals. It is this sharing, this basis for their being a people rather than an aggregate of individuals, that constitutes the beginning point for political analysis.

Essentially a people share symbols and myths that provide meaning to their existence together and link them to some transcendent order. They can thus act together and answer the basic political questions: Through what procedures do we reach collective decisions? By what standards do we judge our actions? What qualities or characteristics do we strive to maintain among ourselves? What kind of people do we wish to become? What qualities or characteristics do we seek or require in those who lead us? Far from being the repository of irrationality, these shared symbols and myths are the basis upon which collective, rational action is possible.

Since these myths and symbols are frequently expressed in political documents, they tend to structure the form, determine the content, and define the meaning of the words in these documents. Voegelin also says that these shared myths and symbols can be found in embryonic form in a people's earliest political expressions and in "differentiated" form in later writings. By studying the political documents of a people, we can watch the gradual unfolding, elaboration, and alteration of the myths and symbols that define them. He calls this process "differentiation," but he also refers to it as "self-illumination" and "self-interpretation."

Viewing the United States Constitution as the critical expression of the American constitutional tradition, we move back in time, seeking the less differentiated, more embryonic expression of what is in that document. Our search takes us to the earliest state constitutions, then to colonial documents of founda-

1. The characterization of Eric Voegelin's theory is taken primarily from the introductions to Eric Voegelin, *Israel and Revelation* (Baton Rouge, 1956), and *The World of the Polis* (Baton Rouge, 1957), vols. I and II of *Order and History*, 5 vols.

tion that are essentially constitutional such as the Pilgrim Code of Law, and then to proto-constitutions such as the Mayflower Compact. The political covenants written by English colonists in America lead us to the church covenants written by radical Protestants in the late 1500s and early 1600s, and these in turn lead us back to the Covenant tradition of the Old Testament. The American constitutional tradition derives in much of its form and content from the Judeo-Christian tradition as interpreted by the radical Protestant sects to which belonged so many of the original European settlers in British North America. Moving forward once again, we find that core tradition being modified, enriched, and differentiated as a result of shared colonial experiences, the influence of English Whigs, the European Enlightenment, and English common law, as well as political events and problems after independence.[2]

It might strike some as peculiar that this analysis of the American constitutional tradition begins with documents from the early 1600s. Prior to the 1760s, there was no "people" that could properly be called American. The colonies were really a collection of peoples, each engaged in a separate process of self-definition. There is still too little appreciation for the historically important process by which these various colonies developed systems of self-government, largely independent of each other, that were highly congruent and surprisingly easy to synthesize into a system. The gradual convergence of a number of peoples into one is too easily explained by a common language, a common background of English legal and political institutions, and a common enemy in the form of a mother country perceived as having grown too domineering. All these factors played a part, but there are also the Judeo-Christian perspective; the colonial charters, which provided for local self-government of some sort; the difficulties of survival, which all the colonies faced; and a shared interest in economic development.

The important point is that, for whatever reasons, from what eventually became thirteen colonies emerged thirteen states with constitutions quite similar in form and content. Even more surprising, there was a common, coherent theory underlying these constitutions. Often referred to by American writers during the founding era as "Whig theory," it had radical variations and more traditional strains that formed the basis for most of the differences among state constitutions.[3] It was nonetheless a sophisticated political theory upon which

2. A summary and analysis of the various intellectual traditions appropriated by American political thinkers can be found in Bernard Bailyn, *The Ideological Origins of the American Revolution* (Cambridge, Mass., 1967). The relative impact of each intellectual tradition is a matter of continuing controversy.

3. For a more complete discussion of traditional and radical American Whigs, see Donald S. Lutz, *Popular Consent and Popular Control: Whig Political Theory in the Early State Constitutions* (Baton Rouge, 1980).

the Federalists in part drew and against which they in part reacted. The American Whigs are known to us today by the name Anti-Federalists, as if they had nothing positive to say.[4] It would be equally fair to brand the Federalists as "Anti-Whigs," though just as inaccurate. As we shall see, the Federalists were deeply indebted to the American Whigs. There are important differences between the United States Constitution, which the Federalists wrote, and the state constitutions drafted by the Whigs, but there are also striking similarities. They are, simply, part of the same constitutional tradition. One can still argue over the manner and extent to which the United States Constitution departs from or fulfills the earlier tradition, but it would now be difficult to sustain the position that the American constitutional tradition begins with the 1787 document.

Even where the U.S. Constitution departs from earlier theory and practice, the reasons are comprehensible in terms of American politics rather than in terms of European logic. The Federalists could not ignore what had come before, nor could they ignore the realities of their political situation. Almost all their highly praised inventiveness went into resolving political problems in ways that were, if not congruent with, at least defensible within the constitutional tradition to which they were heir. One historian has demonstrated how the Federalists had to use, but redefine in subtle ways, terms and concepts borrowed from their Whig predecessors and opponents.[5] The United States Constitution was the culmination of a constitutional experience already one hundred fifty years old, and it derived from but was significantly different from that of Englishmen in the mother country.

In the categories of modern political science, those "influences" upon the American constitutional tradition are the independent variables. What is the dependent variable? The literature on American political thought has been relatively sloppy in this regard. Without a clear sense of what is to be explained, one can too easily link the United States Constitution to many sources that are only generally, if at all, connected with its design and content. To speak intelligibly of "relative influences" upon something, we must first know what that something is.

The simplest way to proceed is to identify some of the characteristics of the United States Constitution that are both typical of and unique to the American constitutional tradition. The list will not be exhaustive, but it will include certain aspects of form, institutional content, theoretical principles, and underlying assumptions that are not part of Americans' British heritage. These will serve as signposts for patterns of development in American constitutional theory.

4. An antidote to this notion can be found in Herbert J. Storing (ed.), *The Complete Anti-Federalist* (7 vols.; Chicago, 1981), esp. Vol. I, *What the Anti-Federalists Were For*.
5. Gordon S. Wood, *The Creation of the American Republic, 1776–1787* (Chapel Hill, 1969), 438–52.

What is American about the Constitution? Just as Americans have no monopoly on constitutional government today, the Founders cannot take credit for everything in their own constitution. Britain taught America the core tradition of constitutionalism. The ancient Greek notion of *politeia,* a plan for a way of life, and the Roman concept of *constitutio* stand as distant progenitors of the modern construction of the term.[6] A host of medieval and Renaissance thinkers contributed to the constitutional tradition upon which Americans built, as did many writing during the seventeenth and eighteenth centuries in England, Scotland, and France.[7] Still, the American synthesis was a unique blend of these intellectual influences and their own inventions.

First of all, there is the matter of form. Britain had a constitution, but the Americans put everything of constitutional status in a *single* written document. It is difficult to overestimate the significance of this practice. The Constitution is thus far more accessible to the average citizen as opposed to an educated elite. Although over time precise meanings will be buried in Supreme Court cases, the basic principles of the political system are readily available to the populace. This aspect of its form, therefore, reflects a strong commitment to broad citizen participation then and in the future. In 1787, Americans assumed that a constitution should take this form, even though they were overwhelmingly of British descent.

Other aspects of the Constitution's form are worth noting. Separate sections define the three branches of government, and the legislative branch is discussed first, as it always is in American constitutions. There is a preamble, but it does not have constitutional status. There is a bill of rights separate from the main body of the constitution but also considered part of it. Americans had a habit of making a bill of rights part of their fundamental law, yet in various ways it was separate from the description of institutions. These and other aspects of form will be shown to derive from American practice rather than from foreign theories.

A second category has to do with the institutions outlined in the national Constitution. Bicameralism was hardly an American innovation, but the American version was neither derived from nor justified by the British precedent. The explicit separation into three branches of government with coordinate powers is not British in origin. The states are mentioned throughout. In order to determine who is eligible to elect congressmen, senators, or the president, we must

6. Charles H. McIlwain, *Constitutionalism: Ancient and Modern* (Cambridge, England, 1958); John W. Gough, *Fundamental Law in English Constitutional History* (Oxford, England, 1955); Graham Maddox, "A Note on the Meaning of 'Constitution,'" *American Political Science Review,* LXXVI (1982), 805–809.

7. Andrew C. McLaughlin, *The Foundations of American Constitutionalism* (New York, 1932); F. D. Wormuth, *The Origins of Modern Constitutionalism* (New York, 1949).

consult the state documents. To this day, the role and functions of state governments in America are a matter of some puzzlement to many Europeans. Americans did not invent federalism, but they adopted it with an alacrity missing in nonmigrating British. The use of different constituencies for electing various public officials departs from the British model, as does the use of different terms of office. The elaborate system of checks, the explicit enumeration of governmental powers, and the creation of an independent judiciary are some of the other elements of institutional design not found in the British model.

A third category involves theoretical principles. Although never explicitly mentioned in the United States Constitution, they underlie and tie together the entire document. These are the principles of a deliberative process, federalism, republicanism, the extended republic, consent, liberty, and a mixed regime. The British were no strangers to liberty, consent, deliberative processes, or mixed regimes. The Americans, however, pursued these principles with a vengeance that transformed them.

A fourth category has to do with assumptions at variance with those underlying the British political system as it existed in the late eighteenth century. The most dramatic involved the way Americans viewed themselves as a people. They firmly believed that on their own authority they could form themselves into a community, create or replace a government to order their community, select and replace those who hold government office, determine which values bind them as a community and thus which values should guide those in government when making decisions for the community, and replace political institutions at variance with these values.

The Americans' rather complete notion of popular sovereignty was also radical in that their concept of "the people" was a broad one. England was the envy of Europe for its liberal institutions, but the least liberal American state in the 1780s, Georgia, enfranchised four or five times the percentage of the population as held the franchise in England. England would have had to enfranchise ten times as many people as it did in the 1780s to match the average in its former colonies. There was nothing else in Europe to compare with the American practice of popular sovereignty.[8] Nor was this a recent phenomenon in America. For all the resonance with Locke's ideas, many of the principles and assump-

8. The percentage of white males enfranchised by colonial and early state laws is still a matter of some controversy, though it is now generally recognized that in America the suffrage was so much broader than it was anywhere else that even the low estimates represent a historical breakthrough. The lowest estimate for all thirteen states combined is around 50 percent of adult white males; the highest is approximately 65 percent. The figures here assume the mean. See Robert E. Brown, *Middle Class Democracy and the Revolution in Massachusetts, 1691–1780* (Ithaca, 1955); R. E. Brown and B. K. Brown, *Virginia, 1705–1786: Democracy or Aristocracy?* (East Lansing, 1964); Marchette Chute, *The History of the Right to Vote in America, 1619–1850* (New York, 1971); Chilton

tions of American constitutionalism were operative before Locke published his *Second Treatise on Civil Government*. In temporal terms, it makes more sense to call Locke an American than it does to call America Lockean.

Sorting out the influences on the origin of the form, institutions, and underlying principles and assumptions of American constitutionalism, we could take the anthropologists' approach. They have taught us that ritual precedes myth, that practices develop and are then justified. Thus we would examine political practices and events out of which constitutional theorizing arises. Certainly we will need to consider this. But in a developed culture, practice will sometimes flow from theorizing based upon earlier practices, and the starting point is difficult to determine.

Historians of ideas would have us trace the origin and development of key concepts and theories, and that will be part of this study. But tracing the development of constitutionalism from classical Greece and Rome to medieval Europe will not necessarily tell us much about American constitutionalism. Even a more modest use of intellectual history has its hazards. Those political scientists writing about American political thought have developed two unfortunate habits. One is to assume that if they find an idea expressed first by a European thinker and then by an American, they have traced the idea to its source. Aside from the obvious possibility that the American might never have read that particular European text, the Americans might be borrowing a manner of expression to explain what they had developed on their own long before the European wrote.

The second unfortunate habit is to seek a single source that was decisive in the formation of American political thought. For example, historians' cumulative work during the past thirty years has rendered anachronistic the view that American political thought derives largely from John Locke.[9] Locke was undeniably important, but there is no single author, let alone a single text, that can account for even a major part of the core of American constitutionalism. We must examine a wider range of texts over a broader span of history.

Williamson, *American Suffrage from Property to Democracy: 1760–1860* (Princeton, 1968); and Lee Soltow, "Wealth Inequality in the United States," *Review of Economics and Statistics,* LXVI (1984), 444–51.

9. For entrée into the extensive literature on this point, see Robert E. Shalhope's two articles, "Toward a Republican Synthesis: The Emergence of an Understanding of Republicanism in America," *William and Mary Quarterly,* 3rd ser., XXIX (1972), 49–80, and "Republicanism and Early American Historiography," *William and Mary Quarterly,* 3rd ser., XXXIX (1982), 334–56. See also D. Lundberg and H. F. May, "The Enlightened Reader in America," *American Quarterly,* XXVIII (special issue, 1976), 262–93; and Donald S. Lutz, "The Relative Influence of European Writers on Late Eighteenth-Century American Political Thought," *American Political Science Review,* LXXVIII (1984), 189–97.

Voegelin tells us to begin at that point where a people first constitute themselves and lay out their political culture in embryonic form. In order to do that, we need to resort to a kind of phenomenological tactic. Imagine, if you will, that you are at a constitutional convention and are in the process of drawing up a document. Where do you go for your ideas? You would probably have read the recognized authorities on constitutional design—your countrymen as well as writers in other nations. But you certainly would have read the constitutions written by your predecessors or by countries whose political systems you admire. Is it unreasonable to assume that those writing the United States Constitution did otherwise? Many at the Constitutional Convention in 1787 had assisted in the writing of state constitutions.[10] James Madison and other participants were familiar with the state constitutions of the 1770s and 1780s and preoccupied with their flaws. As we shall see, they rejected the flaws, not the documents. Those who wrote the state constitutions in turn examined the most recent constitutional documents of their respective states, and so on back to those documents that were the first in their tradition.

In the early seventeenth-century documents of political foundation in America, we find the first expression of a distinctly American approach to the founding and ordering of political society. The foundation elements in these early political covenants, compacts, and charters contain embryonically the form and content of late eighteenth-century American constitutions.

The preceding discussion should alert the reader against expecting to find here *the* origin of American constitutionalism. The seventeenth and eighteenth centuries were a time of extraordinary ferment in political thought and action among English-speaking peoples. To say that political covenants and compacts derived from a biblical model and that colonial charters contain the foundation elements that appear in American constitutions a century and a half later is not a full-blown constitutional theory. The meanings of terms will change, the practices surrounding institutions will evolve, and completely new theories will develop to justify familiar practices. Even so, a systematic examination of the political literature written by Americans between 1760 and 1805 will illustrate the continued connection with early colonial documents.

10. Fifty-one of fifty-five delegates to the convention attended enough sessions to be considered participants in the proceedings. Of those participants, twenty-six had served in state legislatures, most of them having been involved to some degree in the drafting, discussion, and approval of their respective state constitutions. Another six had held major state offices in the executive branch, and at least forty had held some local political office. Their experience in national politics was collectively about the same. Eight had signed the Declaration of Independence; forty-four had served in the Continental Congress. Thus most of them had experienced the debates surrounding the drafting and approval of the Articles of Confederation.

2. Constitutions, Covenants, and Compacts

We must define a number of terms that are not only complex and subtle but changed in meaning since the seventeenth century. The problem is compounded because some documents have characteristics such that more than one term can describe them, even though none of the terms is in the text of the document. Indeed, the English colonists who came to America had no notion that a single document could serve as a constitution, nor did they intend to write one. Yet within a surprisingly short time they wrote a number of documents that deserve to be called "constitutions." We need a benchmark so we can determine which colonial documents warrant being so designated.

Every constitution uses principles of design for achieving the kind of life envisioned by its authors, and the principles will vary according to that vision. This is nothing more, though a good deal less, than what Aristotle said when he characterized the Greek understanding of the relationship between the *polis* and the *politeia*. The *polis* was a way of life, and the *politeia*, or constitution, was the plan for a way of life. The constitution describes what that life should be like and the institutions by means of which will be achieved that way of life. The first description enunciates the values that support the good life, thereby providing a definition of justice. The second includes an enumeration of political offices, the duties of each office, how each is to be filled, how the offices interact to reach collective decisions, and who is eligible to hold office—in effect, a design for the distribution of power.

Essential to that second description is a definition of citizenship, an identification of those holding full political rights. A citizen is one who can take part in all aspects of politics—hold office as well as help determine who holds office. A careful reading of the constitution should allow us to determine the regime in a political system, that is, those who rule. Since the regime writes and approves the constitution, we can expect them to formalize their rule in the constitution, just as the constitution will embody their vision of the good life. Since the constitution will be "directed" by the way of life desired, the specific institutions must be appropriate to the ends sought. The framers must have a sound understanding of the tendencies inherent in each institution.

To identify the regime is also to identify the public, those who stand in a political relationship to each other. In classical Greece, there was a distinction between a people and a public. The former shared in the moral life of the community, while the latter participated in governing. All legal inhabitants of Athens were considered part of the people, but only those with full political rights belonged to the public. Thus, for example, shortly after Aristotle died, full citizenship was vested in only about a tenth of the population of Athens. Most of the rest were freemen but not citizens. A constitution, then, defines both a public and a people, a distinction not as important today as it was throughout most of Western history. Even now, however, those Americans under eighteen years of age are a part of the people but not members of the public. It is also possible, though not necessary, that a constitution will create a new people, a new community, where none existed before. At the very least a constitution must identify the population and the geographical territory to which it applies.

A constitution, by setting forth procedures and publicly recognized political institutions, not only defines a regime but also establishes the regime's authority. In a certain sense, any political system that does this has a constitution, whether written or not, as opposed to a regime that rules through force or through institutions arbitrary in their operation.

A constitution also allocates political power through the distribution of offices and citizenship. First, it defines the range of activities on which the political institutions will bear, in effect providing a definition of the public realm versus the private realm. Second, it determines which institutions have how much say in a given area of public concern. Third, it determines who, as full citizens, will share in the operation of those institutions.

Constitutionalism represents an advanced technique for handling conflict. Since constitutions make clear the locus of political authority and its basis, they provide an efficient means for establishing the third party, government, that can end conflict. The definitions of a way of life and of institutions to further that way of life tend to knit people together, and the overriding sense of community resolves many conflicts. The distribution of power and the limits on its use tend to structure conflict into predictable patterns. The provision of a publicly known, regularized procedure for decision making takes potential conflict out of the streets and into arenas where calm and reason can prevail. Any constitution that fails to manage conflict efficiently and effectively is seriously flawed.

Placing limits on political power is another major purpose of a constitution. This is last, not because it is least important, but because it requires the most explanation. There are at least four senses in which we can use the term *limited government*. The first is the most general: a defined process of decision making limits government. Having decision makers bound by constitutional procedures and the laws resulting from such procedures is often termed the "rule of law." Unrestrained power is the ability to be arbitrary, whereas the rule of law is the beginning of limited power. Americans have developed the concept of limited government well beyond the basic definition, yet this one sense is common in principle to all constitutions. All other notions of limited government result from and are developments upon it. The institution of publicly known, regular procedures for collective decision making, and then writing down these procedures, is the most basic form of constitutional government.

The second sense of limited government involves restricting government to actions that the population has directly approved. Here, the people must give their direct consent on an issue-by-issue basis. The Pennsylvania Constitution of 1776, for example, required that every piece of legislation be passed by two consecutive sessions of the legislature, and the bill had to be publicly posted so that the voters could easily discover what was at issue and quiz their potential legislators during the intervening election. As in the first sense of limited government, there is no limit on the range of issues that government can consider. There is, rather, a limit on the method or procedure used to reach a decision.

The third sense of limited government relates to the content of legislation rather than the procedure for adopting it. As we have seen, the people should be consulted before legislation is adopted, and thus the people pass judgment on every issue. Here, the people seem to have reflected long enough to predict the actions they would prohibit if asked. They can thus codify their prohibitions, write down their restrictions ahead of time in a constitution, perhaps in a bill of rights, or else limit the powers given to government in the first place.

State governments have traditionally relied upon bills of rights to achieve limited government; the national government originally had no bill of rights but did have a limited grant of power. The Anti-Federalists insisted on a national bill of rights as well, and with that addition the United States Constitution combined both techniques for producing limited government in the third sense.

The fourth sense of limited government is even more restrictive. It is as if the people, after long consideration, concluded that some things were beyond even their own power. Whereas some issues are beyond legislative power and rest only in the people, some are beyond popular control. Some prohibitions on governmental activity are thus raised to the status of a higher law. The concept of inalienable rights is associated with this fourth sense, though some constitutional traditions have invoked natural law toward the same end. There are, therefore, at least four broad constitutional strategies available for creating limited government. Writing a constitution implies automatically only the first sense.

Thus we have four possibilities of what will limit government: the legislature's considered opinion of fair process, a majority's sense of justice as expressed in an election or referendum, the considered opinion of a majority or extraordinary majority of the people expressed in a bill of rights or a limited grant of power, or some higher law (for example, God's will, natural law, inalienable rights) as expressed in a constitution.

Following is the entire list of purposes for which people write constitutions.

1. Define a way of life—the moral values, major principles, and definition of justice toward which a people aims.
2. Create and/or define the people of the community so directed.
3. Define the political institutions, the process of collective decision making, to be instrumental in achieving the way of life—in other words, define a form of government.
4. Define the regime, the public, and citizenship.
5. Establish the basis for the authority of the regime.
6. Distribute political power.
7. Structure conflict so it can be managed.
8. Limit governmental power.

These eight purposes provide a good enough characterization for us to determine whether a document deserves to be called a constitution. Together they serve as a benchmark for evaluating the colonial documents that concern us.

A Plethora of Terms

People have a tendency to develop many terms for things that are important to them. Thus, for example, Eskimos are said to have many words for snow, each describing some subtle variation. English-speaking people of the seventeenth and eighteenth centuries must have thought political agreements were of great importance, as they regularly used more than a dozen different terms, sometimes interchangeably, but often to distinguish subtleties.

We need to define with some precision the broad categorical terms covenant, compact, contract, and organic act. Then we need to recover the contemporary meanings of charter, constitution, patent, agreement, frame, combination, ordinance, and fundamentals. Since the colonists were not consistent in using these terms, we cannot conclude, for example, that since an agreement was by definition a form of compact, all agreements were therefore compacts. Once we bring some order to the terms, we can analyze a few documents for foundation elements, formal construction, and the operative terms that describe what they are doing.

A contract usually implied an agreement that had mutual responsibilities on a specific point. A contract carried a restricted commitment, such as in a business matter, and involved relatively small groups of people. It could be enforced by law, but did not itself have the status of law.

A compact, on the other hand, was a mutual agreement or understanding that was more in the nature of a standing rule. If it did not always have the status of law, it often had a similar effect. A compact implied an agreement that in some way affected the entire community or relations between communities. The word's root meaning was knitting together or bringing the component parts closely and firmly into a whole. A compact, therefore, was an agreement creating something that we would today recognize as a community.

A covenant had two distinct though related meanings. As a legal term in England, it referred to a formal agreement that had legal validity under the seal of the Crown, which denoted a serious agreement witnessed by the highest authority. The counterpart to the secular covenant was any agreement secured by God. For example, the formal agreement, made and subscribed to by members of a congregational church in order to constitute themselves as a distinct religious community, with God as witness and securer. A religious covenant thus was essentially an oath, and if it established a political community, political obligation did not rest only upon consent but was secured by the oath. In each case, the highest relevant authority witnesses and therefore secures the agreement. Any compact with both God and the Crown as securer would presumably be both a civil and a religious covenant.[1]

In the seventeenth and eighteenth centuries, a contract was a restricted agreement between relatively small groups of people and did not necessarily have the status of law. A compact was an agreement between a large group of people creating a new community based upon their own consent. A covenant, also an agreement between a large group of people, created a new group of people through their own consent; what made it legal was sanction or witness by the highest relevant authority, religious or civil.

1. For a more complete discussion, see Daniel J. Elazar, "Covenant as the Basis of the Jewish Political Tradition," *Jewish Journal of Sociology*, XX (1978), 5–37; Delbert R. Hillers, *Covenant: The History of a Biblical Idea* (Baltimore, 1969); and Champlin Burrage, *The Church Covenant Idea: Its Origin and Development* (Philadelphia, 1904). On Protestant notions of covenant and their connection with the Hebraic concept, see Burrage, *The Church Covenant Idea*; Peter Ymen DeJong, *The Covenant Idea in New England Theology, 1620–1847* (Grand Rapids, Mich., 1964); and E. Brooks Holifield, *The Covenant Sealed: The Development of Puritan Sacramental Theology in Old and New England, 1570–1720* (New Haven, 1974). For a more general overview of the connection between religion and Western constitutional thought, see Brian Tierney, *Religion, Law, and the Growth of Constitutional Thought, 1150–1650* (Cambridge, England, 1982); and Quentin Skinner, *The Foundations of Modern Political Thought* (2 vols.; Cambridge, England, 1978), Vol. II.

Even with this restricted comparison, a few matters become apparent. First of all, English-speaking people of the early seventeenth century would not have called Locke a "contract theorist." They would have said "compact theorist," and considered the distinction an important one. Indeed, Locke consistently used *compact* to describe the foundation agreement. Second, there was a relationship between a covenant and a compact. Both were based upon the consent of those involved, created a community of some sort, and implied a relationship that was stronger, deeper, and more comprehensive than that established by a contract.

If a people in a given situation had to draw up a mutual agreement but found it impossible to obtain the king's official sanction, they could call upon God as a witness to bind those signing until the royal seal could be secured. If a people reached a mutual agreement that was covenantlike but they chose to call upon neither God nor the king, they must have, for some reason, considered themselves competent to establish the document's force. In this latter instance, legitimacy rested upon the authority of the people, indicating an understanding of popular sovereignty. A compact was just such an agreement. For this reason, Blackstone could say: "A compact is a promise proceeding from us, law is a command directed to us." [2]

Those in a contractual relationship would be inclined toward legalistic wrangling over the meaning and intent of specific words and phrases. The emphasis upon the letter rather than upon the spirit of the agreement would destroy the sense of community as implied by a covenant or a compact and would result in something less—an association for specific, limited ends. True covenants and compacts, without any contractual elements, are communitarian in their orientation, but contractual variants are more legalistic.

An organic act codifies and celebrates an agreement or set of agreements made through the years by a community. In this way, a "common law" composed of many legislative and judicial decisions can be codified, simplified, and celebrated in dramatic form, thereby also renewing the consent-based oaths upon which obligation to the community rests. The early state constitutions adopted in 1776 could be viewed as organic acts as well as compacts, since they usually summarized and codified what the colonists of the respective states had developed over the years.

Colonial examples of an organic act include the Laws and Liberties of Massachusetts (1647), the Connecticut Code of Laws (1650), and the Puritan Laws and Liberties (1658). These acts are long and contain precise terms for limited categories of behavior. Various provisions might regulate behavior in church, prohibit activities after dark, or establish procedures for dealing with Indians.

2. Sir William Blackstone, *Commentaries on the Laws of England* (4 vols.; London, 1765), I, 45.

Highly legalistic, they were after all laws, not contracts, since there was no mention of reciprocal obligations. These are more properly ordinances handed down by the local authority or legislature.

An agreement in the formal, political sense referred to an arrangement between two or more persons about a course of action, a mutual understanding, or a common commitment. The term usually described a document that we would recognize as a covenant or a compact. Indeed, documents frequently used the phrases "to agree," "to compact," and "to covenant" interchangeably. An agreement, at least during the period in question, was far more than a contract. It clearly suggested a relationship that moved beyond the letter of the agreement toward mutual support and pleasure, something close to the "knitting together" implied by a compact or the spirit of community implied by a covenant.

A combination was a bringing together of two or more entities into a whole. The banding together or union of persons was usually for the prosecution of some common, broad objective. The term was often interchangeable with *agreement* and *compact,* and sometimes with *alliance* and *treaty.* As a legal term, it had neither consistent nor widespread use, but American colonists consistently used it as the equivalent of *agreement.* The document later known as the Mayflower Compact, and which was clearly a covenant in form, was known to those who wrote it as a combination.

During the two centuries in question, a frame referred to an established order, plan, scheme, or system, especially of government. It strongly implied a definite form, regular procedure, and order. It also implied change, adapting or adjusting to take into account new factors or conditions affecting but not causing the rejection of the older form, plan, or system. Thus, a frame tended not to be a document of initial founding as much as it was one of refounding, and hence had certain similarities to an organic act. Several times during the late seventeenth century the colony of Pennsylvania reorganized its government, and these documents were called frames in their official titles.

Fundamentals, as in New Haven Fundamentals (1639), were the base upon which to build something. The term referred primarily to nonmaterial rather than physical entities, and thus described leading principles, rules, laws, or articles that served as the groundwork for a political system. Such a statement of principles might be an addition to a covenant or a compact, a preface to a frame or an ordinance, or the agreement itself. Prominent colonial examples are the Fundamental Orders of Connecticut (1639), the New Haven Fundamentals (1643), and the Fundamentals of West New Jersey (1681). As might be expected of a document that lays out the fundamentals of a political system, it looked very much like a constitution; in the case of the Fundamental Orders of Connecticut, it was every bit a constitution.

An ordinance usually was an authoritative command, but had a narrower scope and a less permanent nature than did a law or a statute. The term sometimes referred to founding or instituting something, but in the sense of making conformable to order, rule, or custom—perhaps placing in proper sequence or arranging in proper relative position. It would not be improper to view an ordinance as an attempt to establish "orders" of people according to class, merit, ranking, status, importance, duties, rights, etc. When the words *ordain* and *order* were operative in a document, it was usually an ordinance. Examples include the Massachusetts Orders Devised and Published by the House of Assembly to be Observed During Assembly (1638), which is an equivalent of Robert's Rules of Order, and An Act for the Liberties of the People (1638), which laid out rights in Maryland.

A patent had the root meaning of a public letter or document, as opposed to a private one, usually from a sovercign or person in authority. It could put a contract on public record, command or authorize something to be done, confer a right, privilege, title, property, or office. A patent implied a monopoly of some sort—exclusive use, for example. It was related to a law or an ordinance in that it was handed down by some authority. Unlike a contract, however, it did not necessarily imply reciprocal duties but often simply recorded a grant with no duties assigned the grantee.

The word *charter* is derived from the Latin for a papyrus leaf, a writing, a document. Often this legal document or deed, written on a single piece of paper, confirmed or ratified grants, sessions, contracts, and other transactions. Or it was a document by the sovereign or the legislature to grant privileges to, or recognize the rights of, an entire people, a certain class, or specific individuals. Such was Magna Carta, a charter of rights for the nobility. In his *Leviathan,* Hobbes says that charters are not laws but exemptions from the laws. Charters also granted pardon and created or incorporated boroughs, universities, companies, or other organizations. These written instruments or contracts applied especially to documents or deeds relating to the conveyance of property. The word *charter* was also a linguistic substitute for *privilege, immunity,* or *publicly conceded right.* To say that something was chartered was to say that it was founded, privileged, or protected. Charters and letters patent were similar, though the latter could refer to any authoritative document. A charter was invariably a patent, but a patent was not necessarily a charter. In addition, a charter effectively constituted a contract between the authority granting it and the person(s) to whom it was granted. However, unlike a simple contract, a charter often included many general statements. *Contract,* for example, would not be an appropriate description for a document saying that "and the proprietors shall establish a government whereby differences among the planters may be settled." Virtually all colonial charters granted by the king of England had this sentence or one like it, and on its strength the colonists designed their own forms of local government. A true contract could not have included such a historically important provision. The peculiarity of a charter, then, was that it often contained strong contractual elements linked to many or most of what we would recognize as elements of a founding document like a constitution.

Although rarely found in the title of a document, *constitution* was still a frequently used word in political discourse. Related to the term *constituent*, which refers to being formative, essential, characteristic, or distinctive, it is more immediately drawn from *constitute*, to establish, ordain, or appoint in legal form and status. It was the action of making, establishing, decreeing, or ordaining something, usually by a superior civil or ecclesiastical authority, but at first did not refer to the document itself. A legislature might well issue an ordinance, or an authority issue a charter, in which were the words "do hereby ordain and constitute," meaning that something was being given legal form and authoritative status.

Historically the term had denoted limitations. For example, the Constitutions of Clarendon, a set of propositions drawn up at the Council of Clarendon in 1164, defined the respective limits of civil and ecclesiastical jurisdiction. *Constitution* had described a state's organization, especially the location of sovereign power, as well as the fundamental principles according to which a nation, state, or body politic was organized and governed. For example, there was the declaration of the Estates of Scotland (1689): "Whereas King James the Seventh did by the advice of wicked and evil counsellors invade the fundamental constitution of the kingdom, and altered it from limited monarchy to an arbitrary despotic power." For another, Bolingbroke said, "By Constitution we mean, whenever we speak with propriety and exactness, that assemblage of laws, institutions, and customs, derived from certain fixed principles of reason . . . that compose the general system, according to which the community hath agreed to be governed." [3] These two examples derive from usage fifty to fully one hundred years after the British colonization of North America was well under way, and after the Commonwealth era and the Glorious Revolution, during which much thinking about political foundations took place. Those writing documents of political foundation in the colonies during the early seventeenth century, however, had to use a more primitive formulation.

In summary, *constitution* has to do with making or establishing something, giving it legal status, describing the mode of organization, locating sovereignty, establishing limits, and describing fundamental principles. *Constitution* often occurred in association with law, statutes, ordinances, frame, and fundamentals. It is little wonder, then, that no one at first thought it unusual for legislatures to write constitutions. Although the usage sounds familiar, the various

3. Lord Viscount Bolingbroke, *A Dissertation Upon Parties* (London, 1735), 108.

components had not yet been brought together. Thus, *constitution* might in one instance denote limits but not at the same time describe fundamental principles. Also, the term *constitution* did not refer to a specific document, as we are inclined to do today. When Americans finally brought all the elements together in single documents in 1776, these constitutions derived their elements from compacts, covenants, and charters, as well as from frames, fundamentals, and ordinances. How these elements were developed and blended between 1620 and 1776 is the topic of the next three chapters.

3. From Covenant to Constitution

The year 1640 found fewer than twenty-five thousand Europeans scattered along a thousand-mile coastline. Plymouth colony, comprising seven settlements, had about one thousand people. Those around present-day Boston had about two thousand, with another seven thousand scattered farther inland and up the coast as far as present Maine. Virginia had ten thousand people in the Tidewater counties around Chesapeake Bay; along the Maryland shores were another five hundred. The dozen or so settlements in the Connecticut and New Haven colonies had about fifteen hundred people. The present state of New York had almost two thousand people, most of them Dutch. There were about six hundred blacks in the colonies, a little over two hundred in New York, and about one hundred fifty each in Massachusetts and Virginia.[1] The New England settlements were in some contact with each other, as were those around the Chesapeake, but by and large there was little time or energy for reaching other settlements that were equally poor and too distant for mutual defense. Many were isolated, with all but their nearest neighbors too far for overland communication. Indeed, contact among the major clusters of settlements was usually through England.

Political events in England heightened the colonists' sense of isolation. Not only was communication intermittent, but what there was did not contain much in the way of moral support. The king's precarious political position cast doubt upon the validity of the charters under which the colonists operated. Instructions to the colonies from their respective boards and councils in England were vague, contradictory, and increasingly infrequent. Equally serious, preoccupation with domestic politics interfered with financial support for the colonies. Fortunately, the activities of King Charles between 1626 and 1640, especially the operation of the Star Chamber against Nonconformists and recusants, had

1. Population estimates are from *Historical Statistics of the United States, Colonial Times to 1957* (Washington, D.C., 1960), 756.

encouraged a substantial number of Puritans and Catholics to go to America. Without such "encouragement" the colonies might well have foundered. Even so, the Civil War in England reduced immigration, and in 1645, at the height of the legal confusions, the colonial population was growing slowly, if at all.

The colonists could not rely on theoretical or legal niceties. Their situation was grim. The death rate from disease was high. The plows, planting techniques, and construction methods the colonists brought with them were not effective. Even where the Indians were not hostile, interaction between the two races was fraught with difficulty and had to be closely regulated to preserve peace. Raw materials were plentiful, but labor and tools were in short supply.

Many had migrated in the hope of finding religious freedom, but the king's required oath of fidelity, the colonists' religious diversity based upon minute yet bitterly defended doctrinal differences, and the presence of nonbelievers all combined initially to make that freedom problematic. However, the Civil War in England for twenty years removed oaths of fidelity as an issue, and one faction's moving farther inland could settle doctrinal disputes geographically. Those coming to America for economic gain were initially thwarted by the shortage of labor and the lack of substantial investment—neither of which was forthcoming for half a century. Perhaps only those who came seeking adventure found exactly what they were looking for, but their presence was a constant concern to those who required at least order in their settlements, if not prosperity. For example, the Puritans wrote the Mayflower Compact to bind the settlers to the rules of a community based upon biblical precepts, and thus to restrain the potentially unruly adventurers among them.

The typical charter, and the first, the letters patent to Sir Humphrey Gilbert (1578), required that the colonists pledge loyalty to the Crown, but left the design for local government up to the settlers, as long as local law was not contrary to the laws of England. Although the colonies were usually under the nominal control of a board of directors in London, the grant of local control, the distance, and then the preoccupation with the Civil War gave the settlers considerable latitude. Each colony moved quickly to secure the cooperation of everyone in the community. In small communities, some with fewer than fifty adult males, the members met regularly to plan and make collective decisions. In those colonies based upon joint-stock companies, these meetings resulted because everyone owned some stock and thus had a vote in collective affairs. Regardless, town or colony meetings were with few exceptions a regular event before any foundation document was written and approved. Local self-government came to North America out of necessity, which was soon made a virtue.

The one thing that these largely Calvinist settlers brought with them that was admirably suited to the circumstances was their familiarity with religious covenants as the basis for forming communities. There has been a tendency to focus upon the Puritanism rather than the Calvinism that the many Protestant sects had in common. Although the Church of England initially dominated the southern tidewater, and the Catholics were a substantial minority in Maryland, essentially Calvinist sects predominated in New England, most of the central colonies (including the Dutch, Swedish, and German settlers), and the piedmont region of the South. This fact is central to any explanation of the surprising similarity in the Americans' state constitutions and colonial documents. The Calvinist assumptions and commitments were strongest in New England, and weakest in the South, but they had their effect in all parts of the country.

Early Covenants in America

The appropriation of the biblical covenant idea by the dissenting Calvinist sects and the centrality of religion to their lives are reflected in town records showing that almost the first thing many colonies did was to covenant a church among themselves. One of the first church covenants, that of Charlestown-Boston Church on July 30, 1630, is typical.

> In the Name of our Lord Jesus Christ, & in Obedience to His holy will & Divine Ordinance.
>
> We whose names are hereunder written, being by His most wise, and good Providence brought together into this part of America in the Bay of Massachusetts, & desirous to unite ourselves into one Congregation, or Church, under the Lord Jesus Christ our Head, in such sort as becometh all those whom He hath Redeemed & Sanctifyed to Himself, do hereby solemnly and religiously, as in His most holy Presence, Promise, & bind ourselves, to walke in all our ways according to the Rule of the Gospel, & in all sincere Conformity to His holy Ordinances, & in mutual love, & respect each other, so near as God shall give us grace.[2]

There are five foundation elements in this document. First, God is called on as a witness to the agreement, "In the Name of our Lord Jesus Christ." Second, there is an explanation why the agreement is necessary—the need to create a church in the wilderness to support their living in a manner "as becometh all those whom He hath Redeemed & Sanctifyed to Himself." Third, it creates a people, "We whose names are hereunder written." Fourth, it creates a church. Fifth, it defines the kind of people they wish to become—a people who follow the Gospels and God's ordinances, and who exist in mutual love and respect. This basic form was repeated throughout New England, parts of the central colonies (including the Dutch colonies), and later in the southern piedmont. Wherever dissenting Protestantism went, so too went their church covenants. When it

2. Text taken from Arthur B. Ellis, *History of the First Church in Boston, 1630–1880* (Boston, 1881), 3.

came time for these Protestants to order themselves politically as their charters allowed and as circumstances required, they turned to the covenant form. The Mayflower Compact, signed on November 11, 1620, is typical of these political covenants. Because it already has a certain status among Americans, it is worth examining in light of the Boston church covenant.

> In the Name of God, Amen. We, whose names are under-written, the Loyal Subjects of our dread Sovereign Lord King James, by the Grace of God, of Great Britain, France, and Ireland, King Defender of the Faith, &c Having undertaken for the Glory of God, and Advancement of the Christian Faith, and the honor of our King and Country, a voyage to plant the first colony in the northern Parts of Virginia; Do by these Presents, solemnly and mutually, in the presence of God and one another, covenant and combine ourselves together into a civil Body Politick, for our better Ordering and Preservation, and Furtherance of the ends aforesaid: And by Virtue hereof do enact, constitute, and frame, such just and equal Laws, Ordinances, Acts, Constitutions, and Officers, from time to time, as shall be thought most meet and convenient for the general Good of the Colony; unto which we promise all due Submission and Obedience. IN WITNESS whereof we have hereunto subscribed our names at Cape-Cod the eleventh of November, in the Reign of our Sovereign Lord King James, of England, France, and Ireland, the eighteenth, and of Scotland, the fifty-fourth, Anno Domini, 1620.[3]

The similarities between this political covenant and a church covenant are striking. God is called upon as a witness. The signers state the reasons why such a document is needed, for their "better Ordering and Preservation." It creates a people, all those undersigned, and, instead of creating a church, it creates a government, a "civil Body Politick." They wish to become a people who glorify God, advance the Christian religion, honor king and country, and value justice, equality, and the common good. As a complete foundation document, it lacks only one element—the description of specific institutions for collective decision making.

Since we began with the people of Plymouth, let us follow them to November 15, 1636, when a little-appreciated but historic event occurred. On this day the colony assembled to approve what is now known as the Pilgrim Code of Law.[4]

3. Text taken from Donald S. Lutz (ed.), *Documents of Political Foundation Written by Colonial Americans* (Philadelphia, 1986), 65–66.

4. The original text, written in a tortuous shorthand, can be found reproduced in David Pulsifer (ed.), *Records of the Colony of New Plymouth in New England*, Vol. I, *The Laws, 1623–1681* (Boston, 1681), 6–12. Otherwise, a complete version transcribed into standard English can be found in W. Keith Kavenagh (ed.), *Foundations of Colonial America: A Documentary History* (New York, 1973), 247–51.

The framers' intent was to put all the political practices and institutions, as well as the laws generated since 1620, into coherent form, eliminating what was redundant or no longer needed.

The code begins with readings of the "combination made at Cape Cod the 11th of November 1620" and then of the royal charter, thus establishing the legal basis for what is to follow and turning the entire document into a covenant. The colonists felt compelled to base their authority on a document written in England and on one they wrote themselves. Thus, American constitutionalism derives from charters as well as from documents written in America. The next sentence in the Pilgrim Code of Law has come to be known as the "Plymouth Agreement" (see Chapter 4). The colonists assert that they have the same rights as all Englishmen, and the most important is basing government upon the consent of the governed.

There follows a lengthy, detailed description of political institutions. The document not only contains all the covenant elements, but with the addition of the last foundation element, the description of institutions, the Pilgrim Code of Law becomes the first modern constitution—a constitution that is also a covenant. A free, self-governing people used a deliberative process based upon their consent to create a government. The government was centered upon a representative assembly beholden to a virtuous people as measured by God's law.[5] One hundred forty years later, Americans would use these same symbols as the basis not only for their first state constitutions but also for breaking with Great Britain.

Other early constitutions such as the Fundamental Orders of Connecticut (1639) have similar formats, and we find the church covenant quickly adapted to establishing political communities and developed, by the addition of one more foundation element, into a true constitution.[6] It is difficult to read political covenants from Maine to Delaware until 1645 and not conclude that there was an explosion in political culture of major importance. The colonies were not in close contact. Their points of commonality were the desperate situation in the New World wilderness; the rights and political inclinations of Englishmen but no immediate succor from the distant mother country; the Bible, a close reading of which provided a technique for establishing communities. In less than two decades, these isolated communities evolved a historically important idea—the written constitution, found in a single document and adopted by the citizens through their direct consent.

5. For a similar interpretation of early colonial commitments, see Willmoore Kendall and George W. Carey, *The Basic Symbols of the American Political Tradition* (Baton Rouge, 1970), 56–57.

6. The Fundamental Orders of Connecticut can be found in Francis N. Thorpe (ed.), *The Federal and State Constitutions, Colonial Charters, and Other Organic Laws of the United States* (7 vols.; Washington, D.C., 1907), I, 519–23.

Early Compacts, Popular Sovereignty, and the Common Good

The differentiation of the political covenant into the compact occurred within the same two-decade span that witnessed the differentiation of the religious covenant into the modern constitution. From covenant to compact was a process of secularization. Compacts in colonial America invariably had the same foundation elements as did the religious-covenant-derived political covenants, but lacked only the first element, calling upon God as a witness.

Ironically, the first secularized compact in colonial history originated in a colony whose members were so religious that taking oaths was regarded as tantamount to taking God's name in vain. Calling upon the Lord as witness amounted to an oath, so the people of Providence (Rhode Island) produced a covenant-derived compact, the Providence Agreement of August 20, 1637.

> We whose names are hereunder, desirous to inhabit in the town of Providence, do promise to subject ourselves in active and passive obedience to all such orders and agreements as shall be made for the public good of the body in an orderly way, by the major consent of present inhabitants, masters of families, incorporated together in a Towne fellowship, and others whom they shall admit unto them only in civil things.[7]

Here are the covenant foundation elements, though not the calling upon God, and a few important additions. Political covenants implied all along that the people each had an independent will. Otherwise, the signatures would be meaningless. Without God as witness, the force of the document rested entirely upon the will of those signing. They constitute the ultimate power; the signers are sovereign. This is the first explicit use of popular sovereignty in America. Majority rule, also implicit, was here made explicit. In addition, the last line implies a separation of church and state. Members of a church would run the colony, but present and future inhabitants would join in making orders and agreements for the common good "only in civil things." The symbol of the public good, or common good, which existed in most colonial documents of foundation, is also explicit.

The concept of virtue was central to politics throughout the seventeenth and eighteenth centuries in America. Although the concept derived from two distinct sources, the colonists and later the newly independent Americans for the most part saw not incompatibility but reinforcement. In one sense, virtue meant following God's law as found in the Bible. One who did not lie, steal, or fornicate but who adhered to the golden rule was a virtuous person. The other sense, from

7. This document is in Charles Evans, "Oaths of Allegiance in Colonial New England," *Proceedings of the American Antiquarian Society*, n.s., XXXI (April 13–October 19, 1921), 424. It is also in Lutz (ed.), *Documents of Political Foundation*, 115.

the Greek notion of *aretē,* had to do with those abilities or attitudes necessary to do a certain job well. One who enjoyed physical labor, had a facility with hammers and saws, and had a good eye for right angles was said to possess the virtues necessary to be a good carpenter.

It was an accepted precept at the time that the virtue most vital for a people desiring self-government was their inclination to pursue the common good. To follow self-interest or the interest of a minority was the essence of corruption.

References to the common good or the public good are so frequent, it is tempting to view them as merely pious formulations or, perhaps more cynically, as proof that Americans rarely pursued the common good and thus needed constant admonition. Each view contains an element of truth, but is too simplistic and ignores the historic importance of the formulation. Human nature being what it is, the colonies did not lack people who sought other than the common good. At the same time, the vital need for cooperative behavior among people on the edge of extinction, and the strong communitarian basis of their religion, made the commitment to the common good essential and real. As the threat of extinction and the centrality of religion declined during the eighteenth century, admonitions to pursue the common good did tend to resemble pious formulations. The rise of an individualist ethic, though not nearly as strong in the late eighteenth century as is often assumed, certainly led to a more insistent repetition of the formula as a means of combating the perceived decline in political virtue.[8]

Nevertheless, the commitment to the common good continued to have its effect on the design of political institutions. Perhaps the most obvious was the use of majority rule. John Locke speaks of the majority as the "greater force," and colonial Americans saw majority rule as the only reasonable way to determine the common good. If survival and/or prosperity demanded that the community move relatively free of faction, and repression was rejected as the means of achieving cooperative behavior, then the best choice was to pursue these goals in such a way that most people were in agreement. The colonists were prepared to go in the direction indicated by one-half plus one, but majority rule to them meant more of a consensus than a bare majority. Great pains were taken to generate consensual majorities for various policies. Majority rule and the common good were inextricably linked. The majority expressed its will through a town meeting or an elected legislature. To the extent, then, that either body predominated, the symbol of the common good was still central to politics.

The commitment to the common good was also inherent in the notion of

8. An excellent treatment of the nature of the commitments to virtue and the common good, and changes in them during the eighteenth century, can be found in Melvin Yazawa, *From Colonies to Commonwealth: Familial Ideology and the Beginnings of the American Republic* (Baltimore, 1985).

alienable rights. Over and over again we find the statement that the right to give and withhold one's consent is fundamental. Aside from the rights of conscience and the right to trial by jury, all other rights are alienable "when the good of the whole demands it."

The view that candidates for office should not campaign for votes was also based on a commitment to the common good. Promising differential benefits to certain sectors of the population was a kind of bribery and matched the very definition of political corruption. Instead, electors were supposed to seek out and vote for those most committed to the common good, and thus anyone who campaigned was not worthy of support. James Madison, when he first campaigned for the state legislature, stayed at home. Thomas Jefferson eschewed campaigning when he ran for president in 1800: he stopped his correspondence, lest he appear to be currying favor in his private letters.

The Providence Agreement reflected a commitment to all basic symbols, but the compact form was an accidental side effect of an especially strong religious commitment. Four years later there occurred the drafting of a compact that was not accidental. On October 22, 1641, settlers moving from the coast and up the Piscataqua River (then in Massachusetts, now in Maine) set down the first consciously intended secular covenant, or compact. It is known as the Combination of the Settlers Upon the Piscataqua River for Government, though the original draft probably had no title. There was no minister with this group. Unable to form a church, they wrote a foundation document that in no way resembled a religious covenant. It approximated a covenant nonetheless, but was secularized into what is properly a compact.

> Whereas sundry Mischiefs and Inconveniences have befallen us, and more and greater may, in regard of want of Civill Government, his gracious Majesty haveing settled no order for us, to our knowledge, we whose names are underwritten, being Inhabitants upon the River of Piscataqua have voluntarily agreed to combine ourselves into a body Politick, that wee may the more comfortably enjoy the Benefit of his Majesties Laws, and doe hereby actually engage ourselves to submit to his Royall Majesties Laws, together with all such Laws as shall be concluded by a major part of the Freemen of our Society, in Case they be not repugnant to the laws of England, and administered in behalf of his Majestie. And this wee have mutually promised, and engaged to doe, and so to continue till his excellent Majestie shall give other orders concerning us. In witness whereof Wee have hereunto set our hands, October 22. In the 16th year of the Reigne of our Sovereigne Lord, Charles by the grace of God, King of Great Brittaine, France and Ireland, Defender of the Faith, &c.[9]

9. Text taken from Thorpe (ed.), *Federal and State Constitutions,* III, 1848. It is reproduced in Lutz (ed.), *Documents of Political Foundation,* 187.

The resemblance of this document to the covenant form is obvious. A direct comparison with the Mayflower Compact reveals the presence of all the same foundation elements except the calling upon God as a witness. Even the language and format of the two look similar. It is highly unlikely that the inhabitants on the Piscataqua River had ever seen the Mayflower Compact. The similar form results not from copying but from a common antecedent—the religious covenant. This is apparent in political covenants and compacts written by settlers up and down the coast. Because, as they wrote elsewhere, they were "not yet in a church way" and wished to covenant themselves as a church rather than as a purely political entity, the inhabitants on the Piscataqua chose what we now consider the compact to establish their body politic. Nor could they use the name of the king, since he had not granted them a charter for that part of Massachusetts. In addition, the king's status was at best questionable. Being careful to retain the good will of the king, should he become able to grant the desired charter, these people took it upon themselves to build their own government, a clear act of popular sovereignty.

One can only marvel at the careful, understated language. Few people in our age would be willing to label the circumstances they faced in 1641 as "sundry Mischiefs and Inconveniences." The language does not hide that a free people sought the common good by creating a government, based upon their consent, that would operate according to majority rule. Those living in the British Isles had no need to engage in such an activity—they were already in settled communities. We cannot say, therefore, that these covenants and compacts derived from English common law or the British constitution. Nor can we say that what is recognizably American in these documents was an eighteenth-century synthesis of European Whig and Enlightenment thinkers. In 1641, Locke was only nine years old. Montesquieu, Blackstone, and other writers prominent in the late eighteenth century were not yet born. Operating here were several components of what would become American constitutional government.

Compacts and Federalism

Compacts were used not only to found communities but also to knit settlements together. The Fundamental Orders of Connecticut (1639) established a common government for the towns of Hartford, Windsor, and Wethersfield, while retaining intact each town government. The result was federal in structure without being consciously so. There was as yet no term to describe what the people had done. By 1662 the united colony of Connecticut included Saybrook, New London, Fairfield, and Norwalk along the coast, as well as East Hampton and Southampton on Long Island. In 1643 the towns of New Haven, Milford, Guilford, Stamford, Branford, and Southold (the last was on Long Island) united in a federation known as New Haven colony. In 1662, all but New Haven joined the Connecticut colony, and New Haven joined in 1665.

From March 16 to 19, 1642, representatives from Providence, Pocasset, Warwick, and Portsmouth came together and wrote a compact called the Organization of the Government of Rhode Island.[10] The result was perhaps the first truly federal system in America. This federation became a united colony under the Rhode Island Charter of 1663. That charter and the Connecticut Charter (1662), though officially written in England, essentially ratified the federated governments developed by the colonists.[11] The constitutional strategy of federalism was also evident in the New England Confederation of 1643.[12] The colonies of Massachusetts, Plymouth, Connecticut, and New Haven, each of which comprised several towns that retained their respective governments, drew up and approved twelve articles to govern common affairs. The language and form of this confederation document are recognizably those of a compact.

Thus towns, each with its own covenant or compact for local government, then became part of larger colonies by one of four compacts, and then joined in a regionwide government by another compact. The New England Confederation lasted formally until 1684, though in fact it effectively ceased in 1664. It was the first of many plans for uniting all the colonies. The federal system of 1787 was not newly devised. The relative independence of local government, the states' construction from the bottom up, the states' existence as ongoing governments, and long experience with federalism or confederalism, including the Articles of Confederation, are all part of what made a national federal system both logical and perhaps inevitable.

Covenants and Bills of Rights

The enunciation of values, self-definition, and common commitments was so important to the colonists in America that it came to occupy a larger and larger portion of their foundation documents. The most extensive listing written between 1620 and 1650 was the Massachusetts Body of Liberties in 1641.

The self-definition element in political covenants was gradually differentiated into what we now recognize as bills of rights. The pre-1800 notion of a bill of rights, however, did not include a legalistic limit on the power of government. It was a public elaboration, almost a celebration, of a people's fundamental values, and it put everyone on notice, legislature, governor, and the people at large, that laws and behavior should strive for a certain direction, and action contrary to

10. The document can be found in John Russell Bartlett (ed.), *Records of the Colony of Rhode Island and Providence Plantations in New England,* Vol. I, *1636 to 1663* (Providence, 1856), 111–15; and Lutz (ed.), *Documents of Political Foundation,* 189–93.

11. The Connecticut Charter of 1662 and Rhode Island Charter of 1663 are in Thorpe (ed.), *Federal and State Constitutions,* I, 529–36, VI, 3211–32.

12. For the text of the New England Confederation, see Lutz (ed.), *Documents of Political Foundation,* 207–12.

these commitments should not be undertaken lightly. For this reason, bills of rights written before the national Bill of Rights often contained items that would now appear peculiar. For example, the Massachusetts Body of Liberties has ninety-eight provisions, including the right to trial by jury, prohibition of double jeopardy, and the following:

> 43. No man shall be beaten with above 40 stripes, nor shall any true gentleman, nor any man equal to a gentleman be punished with whipping unless his crime be very shamefull, and his course of life vitious and profligate.
> 79. If any man at his death shall not leave his wife a competent portion of his estaite, upon just complaint made to the Generall Court she shall be relieved.
> 94. Capitall Laws I. If any man after legal conviction shall have or worship any other god, but the lord god, he shall be put to death.[13]

Certainly this bears little resemblance to the purely legalistic bills of rights to which we are now accustomed, but those modern versions are direct descendants of the self-definition foundation element in covenants. The development was a long one. The New Haven Fundamentals (1639), the Capital Laws of Connecticut (1642), the New Haven Fundamentals (1643), the Laws and Liberties of Massachusetts (1647), the Connecticut Code of Laws (1650), the Puritan Laws and Liberties (1658), the General Laws and Liberties of New Hampshire (1680), Penn's Charter of Liberties (1682), the Pennsylvania Laws on Personal Freedom (1683), the New York Charter of Liberties and Privileges (1683)—these and many other examples of self-definition and commitment to values all point to the earlier covenants and the Bible that underlies them, as well as to Magna Carta and English common law.

Once a people and a government have been created, later documents need not do so again, unless in organic celebration. On the other hand, self-definitions and the description of institutions will grow in length, be occasionally altered, and sometimes replaced. Between 1620 and 1787 the last two foundation elements became more prominent, eventually overwhelming the others in terms of the number of words devoted to them. The self-definition and listing of values grew into long preambles and even longer bills of rights. The description of institutions, the longest of all, came to be called a constitution.

These two foundation elements continue to be distinguished in an interesting manner. After a lengthy preamble and a bill of rights, there is often a section entitled "Part II: The Constitution or Plan of Government." Sometimes the last

13. The complete text of the Massachusetts Body of Liberties is in S. Whitmore, *Bibliographic Sketch of the Laws of Massachusetts Colony* (Boston, 1889), 32–60.

section is called a "frame of government." If the institutional description is properly the constitution, then what is the entire document that includes the preamble and the bill of rights? If the constitution is only the last foundation element, then what is a document that includes them all? The answer is, a compact.

The early state constitutions are really compacts in which the constitution became predominant. The institutional description grew so, the entire document was a constitution. That is, compacts literally began to be called constitutions. The people of Massachusetts, in their highly influential constitution of 1780, "establish the following declaration of rights and frame of government as the constitution of the commonwealth of Massachusetts." The preamble did not have constitutional status, but essentially compacts and constitutions became linguistically indistinguishable. Strictly speaking, the preamble should come before the title "Constitution." But placing the word *constitution* before even the preamble completed the identification of compact with constitution. What Americans label a constitution is really a compact dominated by a constitution.

The United States Constitution follows the same pattern. The preamble, which contains the first four foundation elements, follows the title "The Constitution of the United States." But the preamble does not have constitutional status—it is not legally enforceable. A 1978 attempt to incorporate the preamble into the Constitution failed to come out of congressional committee. The U.S. Constitution, then, is a compact dominated by a constitution. As we have seen, compacts are secularized covenants that derive from the biblical tradition. When one reads the preamble, which begins "We the people . . . ," it is difficult not to think of "We whose names are undersigned" in the Mayflower Compact, the first political covenant in America.

[handwritten note:] what g Modeson's attempt to locate rights with text (as is in fact the case)

4.   Charters and the First Constitutions

The development from covenants to modern constitutions began with a highly communitarian perspective and moved toward a more legalistic, contractual view of politics. This shift has been associated with the rise of the last foundation element, the institutional description, to such prominence that it overshadowed the others. That element itself changed, bringing together a variety of threads in one complex fabric eventually labeled a constitution.

At first, there was only a broad, uncomplicated description of basic political institutions. Gradually it became longer, more detailed, and more complete until it included all that we now associate with constitutions—the placement of sovereignty, the definition of a regime, the distribution of power among offices and institutions, and some definition of limits on governmental power. During the colonial era, external documents—the charters, patents, and ordinances written in England for the colonists—dealt with those constitutional functions. Examination of those documents and the institutional descriptions in the first four American constitutions, two written by the colonists and two written in England, will help us uncover the underlying principles of constitutional design present at the beginning of the American constitutional tradition.

The Charter Background

Typically a colonial charter contained the following elements (henceforth "charter elements"): the identification of a grantor; the creation or identification of a grantee; a statement of the reason for the grant; a statement of what was being granted; the license or exclusive use given by the grant; a statement of how the grant was to be administered; specific restrictions or limits on the grant; and the reciprocal duties owed the grantor by the grantee.[1]

1. Most of the colonial charters are in either Benjamin Perley Poore (comp.), *Federal and State Constitutions, Colonial Charters, and Other Organic Laws of the United States* (2 vols.; Washington, D.C., 1878); or Francis N. Thorpe (ed.), *The Federal and State*

The identification of the grantor and the grantee was similar in form to the identification of partners in a contract. Unlike colonial foundation documents in which many people were merged into a new entity, charters explicitly identified two sides, in effect two parties, in a relationship in which they remained distinct. Sometimes the charter formed a number of individuals into the grantee, and to a certain extent this paralleled the foundation documents written in America. However, that single legal entity was formed by and defined by its relationship to the other party in the charter, the grantor. This asymmetry fundamentally distinguished charters from covenants and compacts.

A charter frequently included a history of events leading up to its being granted, which established a reason for its coming into existence, a kind of justification. The charter usually defined a mission for the grantee as well— perhaps exploring or mapping a region or spreading the Christian religion. The result was a rationale that cloaked contract with a tone, a justification, quite different from the simple statement of reciprocal duties. Thus dignity was lent to the effort, and the charter's content became more political than that of a business transaction.

The fourth charter element was the specific grant, usually a geographically defined area. Sometimes the description referred to all the land between two latitudes or between two rivers, and sometimes there were more details. The grant often listed certain mineral and trade rights. The fifth charter element was the indication that the grantee had exclusive use of what was granted and could employ any force necessary to exclude nonchartered persons. This element granted the monopoly that was the usual purpose of charters.

The sixth charter element, a description of how the grantee was to administer the grant, invariably amounted to providing for local self-government within the specified geographical bounds. Institutions, such as a council or periodic assemblies, were sometimes described. More often, an oversight council in England was established, but the colonists could handle all collective decisions, including civil and criminal matters. The colonists sometimes drew up foundation documents because defective or inoperative charters forced them to act on their own; more often they simply filled in the spaces purposely left them in the charters.

The seventh charter element was closely related to the sixth. The grant was limited geographically and by an agreement to share the economic output with

---

Constitutions, Colonial Charters, and Other Organic Laws of the United States (7 vols.; Washington, D.C., 1907). An examination of any of the early charters would illustrate the presence of those elements. The first charter, "Letters Patent to Sir Humphrey Gylberte" (1578), can be found in Thorpe (ed.), *Federal and State Constitutions*, I, 49–52, immediately followed by the 1606 "Charter of Virginia."

the grantor. There were, in addition, limits placed upon self-government. The rules, laws, and ordinances made by the grantee were always to be in accord with the laws of England, which functioned as a higher law. They also required the approval of the grantor or his council in England, who functioned as the final authority. The eighth charter element was often indistinguishable from the seventh: reciprocal duties almost always implied a restriction on the grant. Returning a share of the economic output to the grantor in England was simultaneously a limit and a reciprocal duty.

Although charters resembled contracts somewhat, those operating under the charters, both in America and in England, treated them more as we would treat constitutions today. One does not usually keep rewriting a contract, nor does one include such broad provisions as the charters contained and leave so much to one of the parties. Also, contracts do not arise from or preserve such asymmetry of power. These charters, even though from England, did accustom the colonists to running their own local governments and to doing so within the framework of a document, a charter, that legitimized and limited their political activity. The colonists also learned how to flesh out these charters, thereby developing a sense of what should go into a comprehensive foundation document.

In addition, there were some similarities between the charters handed them and the foundation documents they wrote themselves, at least structurally. The identification or creation of a people parallels somewhat the creation of a grantee. Both provided explanations for the document's being written. Both frequently created a government and described some of its basic institutions. And both were subject to alteration through an orderly process involving reference to earlier public documents. Even so, the charter's basic asymmetrical relationship between the parties differed fundamentally from the community created by foundation documents written in America. That legal relationship injected a letter-of-the-law dimension into the interactions of a people trying to build and maintain a communitarian spirit. With charters, power flowed in one direction, and the parties remained distinct—the operative words were grant, give, order, ordain, establish, confirm, and constitute. These were also in the parts of colonial foundation documents dealing with the sixth element, the description of political institutions, which came to be called constitutions. Constitutions were thus somehow related to these charters, at least in the American context.

Take a charter with the eight elements and replace the king as the highest civil authority with "the people." The people as grantor give a monopoly of political power to governmental officials, who collectively become the grantee, or government. Provide a justification for doing so, and note that the power relationship is asymmetrical from grantor to grantee. Give the grantee the mission of establishing justice, maintaining domestic tranquillity, etc., within a given geographical area. Allow the grantee to exclude any persons from living there without the permission of the grantor, the people. Establish institutions whereby the grantee can make all collective decisions, including civil and criminal matters, as long as the decisions are agreeable to the grantor and not contrary to the provisions in this "charter" that serves as a kind of higher law. In outline form, you have described how a charter lends itself to structuring a constitution with a legally enforceable content and the overtones of a contract.

Take that constitution, make it the last part of a document that begins by creating a people who then agree to form a government, add a self-definition in a preamble and/or a bill of rights, and you have a compact. Call this entire compact a constitution, and you have the basics for the American hybrid—the constitutional tradition that draws upon charters (legalisms, limited government, and contracts) and upon covenants and compacts (communitarianism, majority rule, and popular consent). It is fitting that the first two constitutions in the American political tradition were covenants or compacts written by the colonists, and the next two were charters. All four illustrate the connections between charters and political covenants, and demonstrate the presence of American constitutional principles in seventeenth-century colonial America.

The Pilgrim Code of Law

The document begins, "Whereas, at his Majesty's court held the fourth and fifth of October in the twelfth year of the reign of our sovereign Lord Charles, by the grace of God, King of England, Scotland, France, and Ireland." [2] The manner of fixing dates is similar to that in the Mayflower Compact. That is important, not for tying the two documents together, but for illustrating the consistent use of a formula typical in charters and other documents relating to the king. The colonists carefully and deliberately linked their activities to the monarchy. They operated under a royal charter, which explicitly allowed them to devise and run their own local government. It is one of several examples in the Pilgrim Code of Law in which charter usage and covenant usage overlap. While there were two parallel sets of colonial documents, one written in England and one written in America, they were continuously interwoven. The colonists were subjects of the king, and as independent as they were in the design of their local governments, they still considered themselves Englishmen until the mid-1760s.

The document speaks of "his Majesty's court." The General Court, or general assembly of the colony, derived directly from the charter provision allowing the

2. The text of the Pilgrim Code of Law used here is from David Pulsifer (ed.), *Records of the Colony of New Plymouth in New England,* Vol. I, *The Laws, 1623–81* (Boston, 1681), 6–12.

establishment of local government. The colonists viewed their General Court as functionally equivalent to the English Parliament and therefore not subordinate to it. This is no small matter: one hundred forty years later the colonists would argue that Parliament had no power to tax them since they had their own legislatures under the king. The British would find this argument peculiar, especially given the constitutional changes resulting from the Glorious Revolution. The colonists, rather than being disingenuous, were stating what they had believed all along.

The rest of the first paragraph in the Pilgrim Code of Law explains how at the previous General Court the already existing Court of Assistants (the governor and seven elected members) was increased by eight to form a "committee for the whole body of this commonweal." The committee would review all "laws, orders, and constitutions of the plantation" in order to reject those that were redundant or no longer necessary and codify the rest in a single document. The addition of the eight men, who were mentioned by name, ensured representation for each of the seven towns in Plymouth colony and determined that it would be roughly proportional to the percentage of the total colony population contained in each town.

The eight new men had been elected by the General Court. The Court of Assistants was the elected legislature for the colony, and the addition of the new men created a special "convention" for drafting what would in effect be a constitution. During the late eighteenth century, about half of the first state constitutions were written by legislatures and half by special conventions elected for that express purpose. The committee that drew up the document was half composed of legislators and half of special members elected for the purpose. Further, the state constitutions written by special conventions in the 1770s tended to be in states where many citizens viewed the legislature as unfairly apportioned. Where apportionment was fair, state legislatures could more easily write the constitution. Here the addition of special members was designed to produce that element of fairness, which also approximated equality in the freemen's ability to affect the outcome. This point gives rise to two interesting and important questions.

First of all, why was a legislature that did not necessarily represent every town and that was not proportional to population considered adequate for making normal decisions for the entire colony? Second, why was the body that could make those decisions not considered competent to write this code of law? Implicit in the first question is the concept of virtual representation and a representation based upon the pursuit of the common good rather than upon specific interests. Implicit in the second question is a distinction between normal legislation and the writing of documents of political foundation.

The use of "laws, orders, and constitutions" does not provide semantic equivalents, but rather covers the three categories of items to be codified. Laws regulated crimes and civil disputes; orders governed behavior that was neither criminal nor disputatious, such as the value of currency, the height of fences, and the rights of the people. The term *constitutions* refers to legislation, administrative orders, or customary practices relating to the design and operation of political institutions.

The second paragraph of the Pilgrim Code of Law contains the Plymouth Agreement, only one sentence long.

> Now being assembled according to the said order, and having read the combination made at Cape Cod the 11th of November 1620 . . . , as also our letters patent confirmed by the honorable council, his said Majesty established and granted the 13th of January 1629 . . . , and finding that, as freeborn subjects of the state of England, we hither came endowed with all and singular the privileges belonging to such being assembled; doe ordaine Constitute and enact that noe act imposition law or ordinance be made or imposed upon us at present, or to come but such as shall be imposed by Consent of the body of associates or their representatives legally assembled, according to the free liberties of England.

The first part of the sentence establishes that this document's legal pedigree includes both the charter written in England and the Mayflower Compact, thereby efficiently blending the original charter and the covenant. The second part of the sentence has two important points—the colonists have the same rights and privileges as guaranteed to men in England by the common law; and the foremost right is to have government based upon their consent. The 1629 Charter of Massachusetts Bay, to which the sentence refers, declared that the colonists should "have and enjoy all liberties and Immunities of free and naturall Subjects . . . to all Intents, Constructions, and Purposes whatsoever, as yf they and everie of them were borne within the Realme of England." The Virginia Charter of 1606 was the first to make this guarantee, and similar language would be used in the charters of Maryland (1632), Maine (1639), Connecticut (1662), Rhode Island (1663), Carolina (1663 and 1665), and Massachusetts Bay (1691).

In Britain the most important common law liberty was that taxation had to have the consent of the governed as expressed through an elected legislature. In America this liberty came to mean that *all laws* should be subject to consent—every act, imposition, law, and ordinance. This broader, more active notion of consent, which set the colonists apart from the people who remained in Britain, was a central political symbol in America from the beginning.

The Pilgrim Code of Law established that once a year, originally the first Tuesday in March but later the first Tuesday in June, the General Court convened to elect a governor and seven assistants. The seven were to advise the governor on a continuous basis, meaning that he could call them together daily, if necessary. The governor and assistants together constituted the Council, or Court of Assistants. Their function was parallel to that of a council of selectmen vis-à-vis the town council. The Court of Assistants was in charge between sessions of the General Court but could not make laws. The General Court could be called any time a matter arose that was "too great for the Assistants."

The General Court also elected one assistant as treasurer for the colony and other public officers such as constables, clerk of the court, coroner, and surveyors. The governor could appoint occasional "juries" to carry out needed tasks, such as laying out new roads, and the governor and two assistants could try "trivial cases," those under forty shillings. All trials had to be by jury "according to the precedents of the law of England." Taxes had to be equal, with provision for redress of grievances. Elections were annual. Above all, laws could be made only by the freemen assembled in a General Court.

Considerable space was given to oaths for the governor, assistants, freemen, constables, and non-freemen residing in the colony. Emphasis was upon pursuit of the common good, deliberative processes characterized by discretion, and the maintaining of order. More important, every governmental officer, citizen, and inhabitant had to swear under oath to obey the laws and pursue the common good. The Pilgrim Code of Law thus created a covenant relationship in the colony. Furthermore, the proceedings of adoption clearly indicated that the code was an extension of the Mayflower Compact, which was a covenant.

What are the principles and basic symbols in the code's institutional design? Everything rested upon the consent of the governed, directly implying popular sovereignty. Political equality and majority rule were implied. Elections were central to political operations, and there was some form of representation, though the representatives could not make laws. Since the General Court was the legislature, the legislative clearly was supreme. The powers and duties of those elected to office were specified and enumerated. The pursuit of the common good was paramount, rather than the good of any class or portion of the population. Political processes were deliberative. Aside from the right to base government upon consent, rights surrounding trial by jury were most important. The basic symbols of American constitutionalism discussed earlier all seem to be here, plus a few more.

Is the Pilgrim Code of Law a constitution? Using the list of purposes that characterize a constitution, we can see that the document includes almost all of them. The definition of a way of life was minimal and contained mostly in the Mayflower Compact, which was inserted near the beginning. These were a Christian people pursuing the common good through deliberative processes based upon the consent of the majority. The people were also defined: not only those signing the document, as at the end of the Mayflower Compact, but also those living within the geographical boundaries set forth in the third paragraph.

The process of collective decision making was laid out, political power was distributed (in this case, most remained with the General Court), and the decision-making process was structured to handle the major categories of potential conflict. Governmental power was limited only in a weak sense, by the deliberative process and a few rights. The authority for the regime was established by the insertion of the colonial charter and the Mayflower Compact. The public was defined as all those living within the geographical bounds, but there was no clear statement of how to distinguish a citizen from an inhabitant. That is, nothing was said about how to determine who could and who could not join the General Court and vote. Obviously, from the oath for non-freemen, some resident males were not citizens. So there was no clear delineation of the regime. Aside from these inadequacies, the Pilgrim Code of Law functioned well as a constitution, even though it was a covenant.

The Fundamental Orders of Connecticut

The Fundamental Orders of Connecticut created a complicated institutional structure. To modern eyes it looks more like a constitution than does the Pilgrim Code of Law. Internal references called the document a "combination" and a "confederation," though we recognize it as a compact. The best approach to an analysis is to first reproduce the preamble, since it is largely self-explanatory, and then to summarize the institutional discussion.

> Forasmuch as it hath pleased the Allmighty God by the wise disposition of his divyne providence so to Order and dispose of things that we the Inhabitants and Residents of Windsor, Harteford and Wethersfield are now cohabiting and dwelling in and uppon the River of Conectecotte and the Lands thereunto adjoyneing; And well knowing where a people are gathered togather the word of God requires that to mayntayne the peace and union of such a people there should be an orderly and decent Government established according to God, to order and dispose of the affayres of the people at all seasons as occation shall require; doe therefore assotiate and conjoyne our selves to be as one Publike State or Commonwealth; and doe, for our selves and our Successors and such as shall be adjoyned to us att any tyme hereafter, enter into Combination and Confederation togather, to mayntayne and presearve the liberty and purity of the gospell of our Lord Jesus which we now professe, as also the disciplyne of the Churches, which according to the truth of the said gospell is now practised amongst us; As also in our Civell Affaires to be guided and governed according to such Lawes, Rules, Orders and decrees as shall be made, ordered, & decreed.

The similarity to earlier covenants is clear. These religious people were attempting to live their collective lives according to the "liberty and purity" of the gospel, but they also felt the need for rules of their own. Indeed, in their interpretation, the gospel not only sets forth the ideals of peace and union but also makes an "orderly and decent Government" the necessary means for achieving these ideals. After the reason for the document, and the explanation of the kind of people they are and wish to become, the document then created a people—all those inhabiting the three towns. Each town had a covenant of its own and remained an independent entity. But the new people were not of Hartford, Windsor, or Wethersfield, but of Connecticut. These people formed a civil society, or commonwealth, and then set forth their political institutions.

The first and most fundamental institution they called a "confederation." We might be tempted to call it federalism, and with good reason. There was no explicit division of power between the town and colonywide governments, but the town governments were retained intact and the General Court was given (in section 10) the supreme power of the Commonwealth. Implied here was the very essence of federalism—the preservation of local control, diversity, and the individual character of each component, and the provision for unity on matters where unity was required. The institution here called "confederalism" was one that lacked a precise name in 1639. A century and a half later, Publius would still use the term *federal* as equivalent to *confederal*. Alexander Hamilton says in *Federalist* 9,

> The definition of a CONFEDERATE REPUBLIC seems simply to be, an "assemblage of societies" or an association of two or more States into one State. The extent, modifications and objects of the Foederal authority are mere matters of discretion. So long as the separate organisation of the members be not abolished, so long as it exists by a constitutional necessity for local purposes, though it be in perfect subordination to the general authority of the Union, it would still be, in fact and in theory, an association of states, or a confederacy.[3]

The colonists knew what they wanted to do, and they did so, whether or not concepts and theories existed to explain their creation. In 1639, England had a unitary form of government. In 1639 the English colonists in Connecticut created a federal system. "Federalism" comes from *foedus,* Latin for covenant. The tribes of Israel shared a covenant that made them a nation. American federalism originated at least in part in the dissenting Protestants' familiarity with the Bible.

Daniel Elazar says, "For all intents and purposes, federalism as modern men

3. Alexander Hamilton, James Madison, and John Jay, *The Federalist,* ed. Jacob E. Cooke (Cleveland, 1967), 55.

know it is an American invention." M. J. C. Vile observes, "The United States is a federal country in spirit, in its way of life, and in its constitution."[4] Here is the first of many federal designs made by Americans and their English colonial predecessors. It is in a covenant-derived compact written by a deeply religious people who knew a great deal about the political and religious covenants in the Bible. Federalism is another central political symbol in the American constitutional tradition. Its roots are in covenants, and its expression in America was independent of English common law and major European political thinkers.

The centerpiece of the Fundamental Orders of Connecticut was the creation of a General Court, which was composed of the governor, six magistrates, and twelve deputies. In late spring, all inhabitants (not just the freemen) of the three towns who had taken an oath of fidelity assembled to elect the deputies. At a town meeting, each brought a piece of paper upon which he had written the name of a freeman, the nominee for deputy. The four men receiving the greatest number of nominations became the deputies of that town and were its representatives in the General Court. There was a provision for adding other towns and their deputies.

At the spring General Court, also known as the Court of Election, the deputies elected the governor and the magistrates. Each "ballot" had the name of someone the deputies (and presumably their respective towns) thought would make a good governor. He had to have been previously a magistrate and belong to an approved congregation. Whoever received the most votes was elected. He served a one-year term, and could be governor again, but had to take a year off between any two terms.

The secretary of the General Court then read, one at a time, the names of each person nominated for magistrate at the General Court the previous fall. Every deputy who wanted to vote for the first person wrote the nominee's name on a piece of paper, thereby casting a yes vote. To vote no, the deputy handed in a blank piece of paper for that nomination. The procedure was then repeated until six had been elected.

After the elections were complete, the new governor and the magistrates joined the deputies to pass any laws thought necessary. After the Court of Election adjourned, the deputies returned home until the next General Court in September, but the magistrates stayed to advise the governor as he saw need to call them. On the second Thursday in September the General Court met again. The first order of business was to nominate people for governor and magistrates for the election to be held at the next Court of Election the following April. Then the court considered and passed needed legislation. In April, deputies could

4. Daniel J. Elazar, *The Politics of American Federalism* (Lexington, Mass., 1969), vii; M. J. C. Vile, *The Structure of American Federalism* (New York, 1961), 10.

extend the list of nominees, and the outgoing magistrates could also suggest additional names. The governor and a majority of the magistrates could call additional meetings of the General Court beyond the two required, after at least two weeks' notice. A General Court could also be called by a majority of the freemen, and if the governor did not act on this call, the freemen could meet on their own, select a moderator, and proceed as a General Court themselves.

The oaths of the governor and the magistrates stressed the common good and orderly processes. Several provisions ensured free and fair debate in the General Court. The document refers in several other places to the common good or the public good. The framers were careful to insist that taxes be equally and fairly apportioned. There were no specific rights mentioned. The emphasis seemed to be on the fairness of the process to produce justice.

In the Fundamental Orders of Connecticut, the structure was federal, thereby preserving localism. It rested upon popular sovereignty expressed through majority rule or plurality rule. Giving inhabitants one vote was an expression of political equality, as was the provision for equality in taxation. There was a primitive bicameralism: the General Court had some members elected directly by the people and some elected by the court's "lower house." In the United States Constitution, House members are chosen through direct popular elections, and state legislatures elect the senators in a kind of variation on the system used in Connecticut. There was considerable emphasis upon a deliberative process. The people had all winter to think about nominees for governor and magistrate. There were fail-safe methods to ensure that deliberations could take place even if the governor was recalcitrant. Provision was made for the deputies to be instructed by their respective town meetings before going off to the General Court, and sessions of the court depended on carefully thought-out rules of discussion.

Americans early expressed their concern for political virtue: the higher the office, the more restrictive the qualifications. It is probable that only well-known men would be elected as governor or magistrate. The method of voting was an attempt to ensure a high level of virtue in those offices. The general electorate was broadly defined, though only those with a minimal amount of property could hold office. Americans would keep property requirements to make sure that governmental officers would be virtuous and have a stake in the community's affairs. Seeking the common good was prominent. Representation was clearly a trusted institution. Section ten enumerated powers for the colony government, as well as what amounts to a "supreme law of the land" clause. There is provision for annual elections, central to the early state constitutions, in this document and in the Pilgrim Code of Law.

The Fundamental Orders of Connecticut clearly fulfills the functions of a constitution, though it is a compact. We are already well on the way to differentiating the institutions and principles of constitutional design that will characterize the early state constitutions and the United States Constitution.

The colonists were Englishmen for the most part, and their legal existence rested ultimately upon charters. The seventeenth-century charter, a double-edged instrument, could extend control from England or protect local self-government. Attempts to reassert control—imposing royal charters on all colonies in the late seventeenth century and unifying New England under one charter—were not successful.

Economics, geography, and Britain's absorption in its own affairs and in Continental politics continued to limit the control Britain could exert over its North American colonies. Two of the charters written in the 1660s would ratify the constitutional developments just discussed, and they would survive late seventeenth- and early eighteenth-century attempts to subvert colonial government. Furthermore, these two charters would in 1776 be recognized for what they were—true constitutions.

The Connecticut and Rhode Island Charters

The concept of popular sovereignty was not yet widely accepted in the Anglo-Saxon constitutional tradition, and this renders problematic any claim that the Fundamental Orders of Connecticut or the Pilgrim Code of Law was a full constitution. However, the Connecticut Charter of 1662 used the sovereignty of the British monarch to underwrite or ratify the earlier colonial documents and the form of government they created, thereby sidestepping the issue of sovereignty. The charter reads as if the colonists had dictated it. The king's seal effectively legitimized earlier processes of colonial self-government. By 1776, there was no longer any doubt in Connecticut that the 1662 charter was functioning as a constitution, and that it did rest upon popular sovereignty. This peculiar document thus ended up having considerable historical significance.

The colony of Connecticut centered around what is now Hartford. Settled largely by Puritans from Massachusetts Bay colony, Connecticut was really composed of the three towns of Hartford, Windsor, and Wethersfield by 1639. In that year the Fundamental Orders of Connecticut brought them together in a kind of federal system that created a common government but left their respective town meetings intact. As in the case of Connecticut, most of the towns in New Haven colony had been settled earlier under their respective covenants and compacts, but in 1643 they united in a federation somewhat looser than Connecticut's. Like Connecticut, New Haven had a General Court, which represented all the towns in a common government but left most matters to the individual town governments.

Thus by 1660, the two colonies comprised a number of towns. Both federations had a common legislature that reserved most powers to the respective town governments. New Haven was more of a theocracy, requiring church membership for full participation in political decisions. Further, New Haven denied the right to trial by jury. Still, the similarities far outweighed the differences. And the most important was that neither colony had legal status in England.

The restoration of Charles II in 1660 promised to end the uncertainty that had plagued the preceding twenty years but on terms not entirely congenial to the two colonies. Connecticut quickly sent its elected governor, John Winthrop, Jr., to negotiate. He brought back the charter, dated April 23, 1662, which gave Connecticut legal status as a corporate colony. It also granted to Connecticut the land occupied by New Haven colony.

Most of the New Haven colony towns joined Connecticut, with the notable exception of New Haven itself. Long used to dominating its own colony, New Haven was not keen to become an equal in a larger confederation. New Haven feared having its theocratic style of government undercut. In 1664 the king gave the Duke of York a proprietary grant that impinged on New Haven, and New York threatened to absorb the colony from the west. Faced with this eventuality, New Haven joined Connecticut in 1665. The Duke of York surrendered his claims in return for the towns on Long Island, and Connecticut essentially took the shape that it has today. The colony continued to operate under a form of government that was representative, federal, and constitutional, and had legal status in England.

The Connecticut Charter of 1662 illustrates the convergence of colonial constitutional documents, compacts and charters, into the American style of constitution. The king acted as sovereign in granting the charter. However, it essentially ratified the Fundamental Orders of Connecticut, which was based upon popular consent, thereby legitimating an earlier act of popular sovereignty. In sum, the charter element that identifies the grantor functions as the identification of the sovereign—in this instance unintentionally (on the king's part) blurring the distinction between king as sovereign and people as sovereign.

The charter listed the names of those to whom the charter was given, the elected officials of Connecticut who represented the people. The charter went on to say that all others who were free members of the colony, or who would be admitted as such, held the charter as well. Included were the children of those who were already in the colony or who would be admitted to the colony. By this provision, and the one establishing geographical boundaries, the charter created a people. A similar modification occurred in the covenants and compacts written by the colonists themselves. The charter elements and covenant/ compact elements were in the process of being joined together.

The charter also created a definition of citizenship. The charter was granted to those in the colony as a corporate entity. The charter further provided that certain elected officials *in the colony* would administer the Oath of Supremacy and Obedience to newcomers, thereby making them legal inhabitants. They became subject to the laws made by the colonial legislature; they were protected by the same rights and privileges that existed for older residents. Thus, the creation of a people also defined citizenship, a fulfillment of another function of a true constitution.

The 1662 charter granted the requisite monopoly, but in the context of a startlingly new kind of mission. The grantee was not to explore an area, cultivate it for profit, or Christianize the Indians. The mission was to establish a body politic and operate it by means of specific political institutions. The charter's words are "and are graciously Pleased to create and make them a Body Politick and Corporate." Instead of creating a colony in the classic sense, the 1662 charter created a government. The charter element of assigning a mission was thereby transmuted into the equivalent of the covenant/compact foundation element of creating a government.

Instead of stating how the grant was to be administered, the charter contained a lengthy description of political institutions to be used in carrying out the grant. The result was not only a complete folding of charter elements into covenant/compact elements but also a document that strongly resembled a modern constitution, in which most of the document discusses the last foundation element—specific institutions. The charter looked very much like a constitution, because that is what it was.

The charter also limited the government it created by specifying the boundaries within which the government could operate, requiring that the laws passed not be contrary to the laws of England, and granting the same rights and privileges to the people of Connecticut as were possessed by those still in England. Of course, specifying governmental procedures and processes in a single document accessible to the citizenry also was a form of limitation. Although this relatively weak sense of limited government was not what Americans would often require in their post-1775 constitutions, it still satisfies the requirements outlined earlier for limiting government—one of the functions of a constitution.

The process in Rhode Island was similar to that in Connecticut and produced almost the same result. The town of Providence was founded in 1637 through a compact that the settlers wrote. Portsmouth was formed by compact in 1638. A factional dispute led some from Portsmouth to found Newport in 1639. In 1640, Portsmouth and Newport established a combined government again under another compact. Warwick was founded in 1642 but did not write a formal compact until 1647. All four towns compacted in the Acts and Orders of 1647 to federate a colonywide government that left the town governments intact and responsible for most local matters. The Acts and Orders was a long document that combined a complete code of law with the foundation elements associated with a compact.

The Restoration in 1660 created the same anxieties in Rhode Island as in Connecticut. Through the efforts of Roger Williams and John Clarke, King Charles granted a very liberal charter in 1663. It provided for religious freedom and permitted a religiously acceptable alternative to swearing allegiance. Most important, the 1663 charter ratified the Acts and Orders of 1647, thereby legitimizing the compact-based government built on the consent of the colonists.

The Rhode Island Charter differed little from the Connecticut Charter granted the year before. All that has been said here about the latter can be said about the former as well. The Rhode Island Charter differs in that it was much wordier, contained a tortuously detailed explanation of why a charter was needed, and discussed religious freedom at length.

The explanation and the discussion were a kind of preamble, and then the charter got down to the business of creating a government and describing its institutions. The early state constitutions written more than a century later would frequently include a long preamble explaining why the document was necessary and a bill of rights. The discussion in the 1663 charter about religious liberty used language similar to that in the early state constitutions. The Rhode Island Charter, to the extent it differs from the Connecticut Charter, looked even more like an early state constitution, which, in 1776, it became.

The Pilgrim Code of Law, the Fundamental Orders of Connecticut, the Connecticut Charter of 1662, and the Rhode Island Charter served effectively as colonial constitutions, and the latter two as proper state constitutions as well. This necessarily brief discussion does not follow the development in Massachusetts as closely, though the pattern—from compact to charter to constitution—was similar. These three states had the closest relationship between colonial documents and the early state constitutions: each state's colonial charter, directly based upon earlier compacts written by colonists, served as the initial state constitution in 1776. Other states wrote new constitutions in the 1770s, but they also drew heavily upon their respective colonial experience and institutions.

In American constitutionalism, there was more continuity and from an earlier date than is generally credited. The early state constitutions did not suddenly spring into being. Neither did the United States Constitution. The continuity was rooted not only in documents and institutions but also in a way of viewing and approaching politics.

5. Constitutional Development During the Colonial Era

Between 1578 and 1725 the constitutional theory evolving in British North America was a concatenation or interpenetration of charters and rules made in England, political ideas and instruments generated by the colonists themselves, English common law, and a developing theory of the colonies' place in the British political system. The manner in which these influences mixed and grew was different in the various clusters of colonies. The result was three broad "subcultures" within American constitutionalism. Their political development can, at the risk of oversimplification, be related to some basic differences in their history, geography, and demographics, just as the growth of a reasonably common political culture can be traced to some decisive similarities in the circumstances of all colonies.

Colonization began in the South and, despite an initial setback, developed rather quickly. Virginia defined the southern pattern. Initially founded by a trading company, it became in 1624 the first royal colony. By 1776, all land south of Virginia would be royal colonies based upon the Virginia model. Virginia most resembled England in its social structure. The Church of England was the established church for a number of years, and there were large landowners and thus a system that seemed at first glance similar to England's class structure. Aside from Charleston and Savannah, there were relatively few towns of any size in the South. The area looked, in short, much like the England centered on the shire or county government.

However, the South still had a number of important similarities with the rest of America. There was in fact no true aristocracy. The size and wealth of the middle strata far exceeded anything found in England. The upper class did not own or claim most of the land as the aristocracy did in England. The large landowners worked hard to maintain social distance from other Virginians, but their political interests vis-à-vis England were similar to those of middling wealth in America, a fact reflected in the operation of the colonial legislature.

The governor almost always picked the wealthier and more influential plant-ers to serve on the Privy Council, which became a miniature upper house—a pale copy of the House of Lords. As in England, money to run the government came from taxes voted by the lower house, the House of Burgesses. But circum-stances in America transformed the operation of what looked to be a typically British legislature. A pattern of uneasy cooperation and frequent conflict char-acterized the relationship between governor and burgesses, with the council more often than not supporting the House of Burgesses. Without the automatic support of the "better sort," the governor lacked the political base to successfully oppose the burgesses' attempts to gain political dominance. Conflict often led the governor to dismiss the legislature (which he had every right to do) and maintain his position with his own money and with funds found elsewhere.

The difference in the legislature's operation had to do with another English practice brought to America and transformed. Since the 1400s the right to vote in England had been granted to all those who owned enough land to earn at least forty shillings a year rent, usually between forty and sixty acres. In England, where a relatively small number of men were landowners, this rule enfran-chised from 2 percent to 6 percent of the adult males. In America, with plentiful land and no ancient feudal claims, the same rule enfranchised 25 percent to 35 percent of white, adult male Virginians. Although that figure was low by Ameri-can standards (the percentage became higher the farther north one went), it nevertheless was a striking alteration of English political reality. Furthermore, the governor was isolated from England by the Atlantic Ocean, had few troops available to him (most of which were colonial militia anyway), and had a council disposed to support the House of Burgesses. These and other aspects of south-ern political life conspired to move constitutional development in a direction similar to, though distinguishable from, that found in the North.

New England developed governments that were more independent of En-gland and more divergent from the English model. Although by 1776 a royal colony, Massachusetts was begun by a trading company; for seventy years, it functioned almost as if it were independent. When, in 1691, England ordered Plymouth colony merged with Massachusetts Bay colony, the combination maintained that strong tradition of self-government. Massachusetts, for exam-ple, used its charter of 1691 as a functioning constitution from 1776 to 1780 without readoption or alteration. In 1776 the people of Massachusetts simply acted as if they had been independent all along. New Hampshire and Maine were part of colonial Massachusetts and would later be essentially extensions of its political culture. Connecticut and Rhode Island became, through their charters from the 1660s, self-governing colonies.

Although economic opportunity was part of the motivation for settlement of New England, there were those who sought religious freedom. The population

[handwritten note: l.e. not of qu...]

was heavily middle class in economic origins and orientation, and consisted mainly of dissenting Protestants of a radical Calvinist bent. Although many sects existed, the Calvinist base, and the common desire to involve the congregations in the running of the churches, strongly colored New England politics. That desire and the joint-stock companies led to a stronger adherence to majority rule and a broader suffrage than existed elsewhere in the colonies. The emphasis on religion meant a stronger sense of community and a greater willingness to legislate on morals, economic practices, and day-to-day behavior. Reinforcing these characteristics was the terrain, which forced the inhabitants to settle in pockets and thus live in towns.

The colonies between New England and the South developed at least half a century later. By 1776, New Jersey and New York were royal colonies, but their proprietary roots were still strong. Pennsylvania, Delaware, and Maryland were still proprietary. The most striking aspect of the middle colonies was the diversity in their respective populations. New York had a strong Dutch presence, as did northern New Jersey and Delaware. Delaware had many Swedes. Pennsylvania had many Germans—in 1776, when Pennsylvania published twenty-five thousand copies of the new state constitution, one-third were printed in German.

The middle colonies also had greater religious diversity. All the Protestant sects found in New England were there as well. The Germans, Swedes, and Dutch were members of the Protestant community, which included large numbers of Anabaptists who were not always welcome in colonies to the north and south. Another group not always welcome in New England, the Quakers, were prominent in Philadelphia politics. Finally, Maryland had originally been settled by Catholics, and though they were a minority in Maryland by 1776, they were conspicuous by their relative absence in New England and the South.

Compared to the other two sections, the middle colonies had more heterogeneous populations, relied more on export and trade, were more urbanized, and were less concerned with preserving religious or social structures. The two largest cities and economic centers in 1776 were Philadelphia and New York, and the middle states together contained approximately two-thirds of all urbanized Americans (those in cities of more than twenty-five hundred). In matters of religion, Maryland and Pennsylvania especially granted freedom of worship early on. The ethnic diversity helped create, and then fed, a greater concern for economic development than for religious, ethnic, or class hegemony. Those seeking economic opportunity as individuals were more likely to be attracted to the middle colonies.

One should not push the differences too far. By 1776, there was a common core to all three political subcultures. At the same time, their several origins and experiences produced recognizable variants in constitutional design at the state level. Elazar has characterized the three variants as "moralistic" in New England, "individualistic" in the middle colonies, and "traditionalistic" in the South. He is at pains to stress that the identifiable differences are more a matter of emphasis and degree, since those characteristics are present, to a greater or lesser extent, in all three regions.

A Moralistic Political Subculture

The moralistic political culture emphasizes the commonwealth conception as the basis for democratic government. Politics, to the moralistic political culture, is considered one of the great activities of humanity in its search for the good society—a struggle for power, it is true, but also an effort to exercise power for the betterment of the commonwealth. Consequently, in the moralistic political culture both the general public and the politicians conceive of politics as a public activity centered on some notion of the public good and properly devoted to the public interest. . . . Since the moralistic political culture rests on the fundamental conception that politics exists primarily as a means for coming to grips with the issues and public concerns of society, it also embraces the notion that politics is ideally a matter of concern for every citizen, not just for those who are professionally committed to political careers. Indeed, it is the duty of every citizen to participate in the political affairs of the commonwealth.[1]

Most of those who migrated to New England sought religious freedom, though there were adventurers and seekers of economic gain as well. The content of their dissenting religious beliefs, their tendency to migrate in groups, and their practice of resolving collective problems, both religious and secular, by consulting the entire community, all led to the strong communitarian basis of New England politics. Colonial political documents, as well as early New England state constitutions, reflected moralistic communitarianism. For example, even though some settlements linked the right to vote and church membership, in general the rate of suffrage was high for the time. Also important was a local majority's close control of elected officials.

Not only was there a broad definition of suffrage in New England, but people were expected to contribute their time and their talents to their community. In addition to voting, sitting on juries, and attending town meetings, citizens ran for and served in an astonishing variety of elective offices. Many towns had so many, there were not always enough people available to fill them.[2]

1. Daniel J. Elazar, *American Federalism: A View from the States* (3rd ed.; New York, 1984), 117–18.

2. Jack P. Greene (ed.), *Settlements to Society, 1607–1763* (New York, 1975), 249; George E. Howard, *An Introduction to the Local Constitutional History of the United States* (Baltimore, 1889), 91; John Fairfield Sly, *Town Government in Massachusetts (1620–1930)* (Cambridge, Mass., 1930), 76.

Towns were the basic political unit, and all New England colonies, and thus states, were built from federations of towns. Their early state constitutions would provide for what we today call "local control" by town government, and representation in the legislatures would be essentially by towns rather than by number of individuals. Still, their religious beliefs gave them a strong sense that all persons were equal in the exercise of free will, and serious effort would be made to represent towns in rough proportion to the number of resident individuals. The early state constitutions, however, protected the rights of local communities rather than the rights of the individuals within them.

Bills of rights would be extensive, and they would resemble admonitions to seek perfection rather than actually limit government. The state constitutions in New England were closest in content and form to the earlier covenants and compacts. The basis for legislative supremacy, the control over the legislatures exercised by local majorities, the form and justification for bicameralism, and the rhetoric of liberty, all reflected the dissenting Protestant background that predominated in New England. This moralistic communitarianism was similar to the political ideology of the Commonwealth period in England, though without a strong leader such as Cromwell. New England most strongly appropriated the commonwealth tradition. Historians who see that tradition as fundamental to early American politics do so invariably on the basis of New England writings.

At the same time, dissenting Protestant theology carried with it the seeds of individualism and a more radical egalitarianism, even if these were not dominant before the nineteenth century. The New England religious background carried also the basis for a highly successful commercialism. Economic success could be a sign of virtue and thus of being among the elect. The frugality, delayed gratification, hard work, simple tastes, and inclination to accumulate were part of the triumph of the "Yankee trader." Although moralistic communitarianism was dominant in New England, there were also strong affinities with the "individualistic" pattern found in the middle colonies.

An Individualistic Political Subculture

The individualistic political culture emphasizes the conception of the democratic order as a marketplace. In this view, government is instituted for strictly utilitarian reasons, to handle those functions demanded by the people it is created to serve. A government need not have any direct concern with questions of the good society, except insofar as it may be used to advance some common conception of the good society formulated outside the political arena just as it serves other functions. . . . In general, government action is to be restricted to those areas, primarily in the economic realm, that encourage private initiative and widespread access to the marketplace. . . . Since the individualistic political culture eschews ideological concerns in its businesslike conception of politics, both politicians and citizens look upon political activity as a specialized one, essentially the province of professionals, of minimum and passing concern to the lay public, and with no place for amateurs to play an active role.[3]

The middle colonies basically developed after the 1680s. By then, mercantilism was emerging in British colonial affairs, and the middle colonies experienced rapid growth as both capital and labor flowed to the New World. Boston, Savannah, and Charleston benefited from this influx, but New York, Philadelphia, and Baltimore and the middle colonies in general benefited the most. In 1660 the middle colonies had only one-seventh the population of either New England or the South (only 7 percent of all colonists). By 1776, they would together achieve near parity with the other two areas, each region having one-third of the total American population. Over a span of seventy-five years, beginning in 1700, the middle colonies grew at twice the rate of New England or the South.[4]

The middle colonies tended to attract individuals rather than groups, and thus saw somewhat less emphasis on coherent communities. Catholics came to Maryland for religious freedom. William Penn established Pennsylvania as a haven for religious minorities. As a result, Pennsylvania attracted the largest non-British population—Germans from the Rhineland-Palatinate—whose dissenting Protestant beliefs had brought them persecution. The Quakers were largely excluded from New England and the South. The Pennsylvania Dutch, Mennonites, and Amish today remind us of the extent to which the middle colonies also served as the home for religious communities.

Still, on balance, the large cities and rapid economic growth attracted a more economically oriented, individualistic sort of settler. In many respects, New York, Pennsylvania, New Jersey, Delaware, and the western part of Maryland most resembled the pluralistic, dynamic, commercial America of today. In New York and Philadelphia were many men, like Benjamin Franklin and Alexander Hamilton, who wrote and acted in a more capitalistic way. They would readily respond to Adam Smith and the Scottish philosophers writing on free enterprise. Perhaps it is no accident that James Madison was exposed to the writers of the Scottish Enlightenment, especially Hume and Ferguson, while attending college in New Jersey rather than while growing up or living in Virginia.

The 1777 New York Constitution stands as the most no-nonsense document of the era.[5] Spare, free of hortatory and moralistic baggage (the Declaration of

3. Elazar, *American Federalism,* 115–17.

4. These and other demographic data on colonial America are taken from Greene (ed.), *Settlements to Society,* esp. 238–39.

5. Francis N. Thorpe (ed.), *The Federal and State Constitutions, Colonial Charters, and Other Organic Laws of the United States* (7 vols.; Washington, D.C., 1907), V, 2623–38.

Independence is the preamble), it had a straightforward description of a political system that minimized government intervention. The document also reflected more of an openness to innovative political forms than was the case in New England and the South.

In the 1776 Pennsylvania Constitution were provisions for a unicameral legislature, the majority's control of that body, and the Council of Censors, an institution independent of traditional political forms in America. Pennsylvanians' commitment to rational calculation and political principle would make the moralistic New Englanders uneasy, and their innovativeness would puzzle the traditionalistic southerners. Even Maryland, with its electoral college to select members to its senate, caught the spirit of innovation.[6]

Once again it was a matter of emphasis. Philadelphia and New York City had their traditionalistic tendencies, not to mention the patroon system in upstate New York, just as religious minorities in the middle colonies brought the moralistic political culture to bear. Still, the openness to individualism, commercialism, utilitarianism, and the Enlightenment marked this region. Given the acceptance of Adam Smith's and David Hume's view of politics, it is not accidental that writings by the middle colonies' leaders reveal the strong influence of the Scottish Enlightenment.

A Traditionalistic Political Subculture

The traditionalistic political culture is rooted in an ambivalent attitude toward the marketplace coupled with a paternalistic and elitist conception of the commonwealth. It reflects an older, precommercial attitude that accepts a substantially hierarchical society as part of the ordered nature of things, authorizing and expecting those at the top of the social structure to take a special and dominant role in government. Like its moralistic counterpart, the traditionalistic political culture accepts government as an actor with a positive role in the community, but tries to limit that role to securing the continued maintenance of the existing social order. To do so, it functions to confine real political power to a relatively small and self-perpetuating group drawn from an established elite. . . . [T]hose who do not have a definite role to play in politics are not expected to be even minimally active as citizens. . . . Practically speaking, the traditionalistic political culture is found only in a society that retains some of the organic characteristics of the preindustrial social order.[7]

Virginia and the other southern colonies were originally settled using a hierarchical form of organization. Although the first general assembly in America

6. *Ibid.*, V, 3081–92, III, 1686–1712.
7. Elazar, *American Federalism*, 118–19.

met in Virginia, its politics was heavily marked by the role of the military, large landholders, and the Church of England. The Virginia charters were given to the likes of Sir Humphrey Gilbert and Sir Walter Raleigh, who might be termed gentlemen-adventurers of the English aristocracy. The first laws in Virginia were the "Articles, Laws, and Orders, Divine, Politic, and Martial for the Colony of Virginia" (1610–11), written by Sir Thomas Gates, Knight, Lieutenant-General; and approved by Sir Thomas West, Knight, Lord Governor, and Captain-General; again enlarged by Sir Thomas Dale, Knight, Marshall, and Deputy-Governor. It is clear that something was going on here at odds with the covenant/compact documents being written by the colonists in New England.[8]

The "Articles, Laws, and Orders" was a list of commands from the military governor that dealt with almost every form of action in the colony. Its intent was to bring order and discipline, and it dealt harshly with infractions. In 1619 the first General Assembly of Virginia passed several laws also notable for relentless attention to the preservation of order. They began with idleness, gaming, drunkenness, and "excess in apparel" and moved on to the conversion of Indians, requiring every settler to plant certain crops and trees, etc. This was a general assembly and so was an example of the colonists collectively making their own laws, but the tone differs markedly from that of New England documents.

The southern colonies were an attempt to transplant the English country culture. That was doomed to failure, since the aristocracy did not migrate to America and since plentiful land in America quickly led to the formation of a substantial yeoman class. The Church of England fared little better. Even the southern colonies tended to draw more Dissenters than Church of England members. Finally, since the charters for the southern colonies also provided for local government and transferred the common law, military control could not be maintained. The meeting of the 1619 assembly marked the end of military organization in the colony.

Even so, the prominence of some planters, the initial form of organization, and the dispersal of the population over counties (rather than concentration in easily organized towns) led to a traditionalistic variant of American political culture. The politics of deference was much stronger in the South, government was by and large in the hands of a relative few of the "better sort," and the emphasis in politics was on the preservation of the existing order rather than on commercial development or the pursuit of communities based upon higher political principles, religious or rationalistic. In effect, while New England attracted a post-medieval, bourgeois population, the South was preserving a

8. The text is in Merrill Jensen (ed.), *English Historical Documents: American Colonial Documents to 1776* (12 vols.; New York, 1955), IX, 1869–1976. It is also in Donald S. Lutz (ed.), *Documents of Political Foundation Written by Colonial Americans* (Philadelphia, 1986), 55–63.

milder, modified form of precommercial, traditional society based upon English county politics built around the country manor house and feudal relations.

The southern state constitutions of the 1770s and 1780s defined an electorate that was broader than the one in England but was less than half that in New England. Conditions in America did not permit a medieval pattern of serfdom to support the paternalistic social, economic, and political elites, so the institution of slavery, which substituted for the serfs, had to have legal protection.

Charleston and Savannah became ports and commercial centers of some importance, but the southern ambivalence to the marketplace continued until the Civil War and even beyond. The southern elites fought a rearguard action against the demand for political equality by the increasing numbers of settlers in the piedmont regions. Not only did they thus threaten the predominance of the planter elites, they belonged heavily to the dissenting Protestant denominations. Giving them fair representation meant the disestablishment of the Church of England in the South. The political rise of the piedmont areas moved the South much closer to the political values and institutions of the other colonies by the time of the Revolution. The individualistic and moralistic strains of American political thought left their mark on the early state constitutions of Virginia and the Carolinas, but the trend in the South remained more traditionalistic than it was in the other two regions.

Each cluster of colonies exhibited a tendency toward one of the three cultures outlined by Elazar, but characteristics of all three could be found in all colonies, and the constitutional tradition of America is an amalgam. The notion of a commonwealth would be as understandable in colonial Virginia and Pennsylvania as in Massachusetts. The famous Yankee trader was as inclined toward individualism and commerce as was his counterpart in New York and the southern seaports. Social elitism could be found in Boston and Philadelphia as well as in Richmond and Savannah.

Magna Carta and the Common Law

The colonial charters invariably contained another constitutionally important provision in addition to allowing the colonists to build their own local government. The Virginia Charter of 1606 says:

> [A]ll and everie the parsons being our subjects which shall dwell and inhabit within everie or anie of the saide severall Colonies and plantacions and everie of theire children which shall happen to be borne within the limitts and precincts of the said severall Colonies and plantacions shall have and enjoy all liberties, franchises and immunities within anie of our other dominions to all intents and purposes as if they had been abiding

and borne within this our realme of Englande or anie other of our saide dominions.[9]

The phrase "all liberties, franchises and immunities" conveyed to the citizens of the New World the English common law, including the provisions of Magna Carta. Unlike the colonists in French or Spanish settlements in America, English colonists were full citizens even though away from the mother country. It is difficult to overestimate the importance of this fact. The British government later argued that the common law did not apply in America, but the colonists insisted that the common law was theirs. The Americans, however, were selective: sometimes they argued that only the common law in effect prior to their emigration belonged to them, sometimes that all common law up to independence was theirs. They ignored the parts of Magna Carta and the common law that dealt with feudal structures, the establishment of the Anglican church, and anything else not in line with their preferences.

Virginia and Maryland had a strong common law basis to their respective legal systems from the beginning. The New England colonies initially preferred biblical sources, but their charters also implied strong ties with the common law. The middle colonies were less inclined to accept the common law of England. Nevertheless, they too managed to appropriate much of it. Starting from very different historical, social, and political circumstances, the colonies wove common law into their respective political traditions, and they all appropriated, or failed to appropriate, approximately the same parts of it.

What, precisely, was appropriated? One way to answer the question is to focus upon the parts of Magna Carta that were consistently used in colonial political systems. Until just before the Revolution, Coke's commentaries were the summaries of the common law. Coke, in turn, drew heavily upon Magna Carta as the centerpiece of English common law.[10]

From Magna Carta the colonists took the fundamental principle of no taxation without consent. This was narrower than their own belief that all government should rest upon consent. It is a prime example of how they borrowed from common law on the basis of what was congruent with or supported their broader commitments. The colonists also appropriated the basic constitutional principle of the rule of law, which implied that all people, including rulers, are bound by certain legal restrictions. Part of the common law legacy to American constitu-

9. Thorpe (ed.), *Federal and State Constitutions*, I, 52–55.

10. A. E. Dick Howard, *The Road From Runnymede: Magna Carta and Constitutionalism in America* (Charlottesville, 1968), 116–32, 265–74. Much of the discussion of common law is based on Howard's work, though it should be noted that Howard credits Magna Carta with more influence on American constitutionalism than does this study.

tionalism, and perhaps its most important contribution, was the idea of limited government. However, the English notion encompassed only the weakest of the four senses of limited government: everyone was supposed to be subject to the same legal processes. Americans, on the other hand, believed that the majority was the source of law and that thus government was limited by majority will. There was little sense until the 1780s that the majority could also be bound by fundamental law.

The most profound effect of common law was not in principles of constitutional design or in generating the basic sense of what a constitution is. Americans used it to generate the core of their bills of rights: the right to trial by a jury of one's peers; the right to a speedy trial; prohibition of bills of attainder, *ex post facto* laws, and cruel and unusual punishment; the guarantee of habeas corpus; the rights of widows and the poor; the right to compensation for the taking of private property; and equal protection under the laws. Also taken from the common law was the notion that a judge should not have an interest in any case upon which he sits in judgment. This led to a primitive version of the separation of powers in the sense of prohibiting those in government from holding several offices at once.

These rights and legal principles existed in bills of rights throughout the colonial era, as well as in the early state constitutions. However, bills of rights were often not looked upon as part of a constitution or as having constitutional status. During the colonial era we typically find what amounts to a bill of rights embedded in a code of law written and/or approved by the legislature.

For example, the Massachusetts Body of Liberties (1641) codified and summarized the previous twenty years of legislation in the colony and added a number of new "liberties." Few people today would recognize even a resemblance to a bill of rights, yet it was perhaps the first in America. Most of its provisions dealt with defining categories of crime and the punishment each deserved. By writing down such definitions and punishments, the authors effectively created a bill of rights. First of all, the public listing of criminal behavior implicitly guaranteed that behavior not so proscribed was acceptable. It minimized the possibility of arbitrary arrest. Also, by stating the punishment for each crime, the Body of Liberties created a rough social equality. With only a few exceptions ("gentlemen" would sometimes be fined rather than receive lashes), everyone who committed a given crime would have the same punishment. In general, cruel and unusual punishments were eliminated as well. There were also recognizable rights pertaining to strangers and foreigners, indentured servants, widows and orphans, and children and women in general. Such rights might derive indirectly from the common law, since there were a number of similarities. However, the people of New England tended to rely upon the Bible for such things, and the similarity with the common law may reflect the biblical prescription in English common law as well.

These early codifications of laws functioned not only as bills of rights but also as major documents of self-definition. At first, the foundation element of self-definition was just one part of a complete foundation document, such as the Mayflower Compact. However, the matter of self-definition was so important to colonial Americans that it came to occupy longer portions of foundation documents and sometimes even a separate document.

The Pilgrim Code of Law (1636), for example, listed a number of values and rights within the body of what is otherwise a constitution, including the right to trial by jury and a commitment to equal taxation. The 1638 Act for the Liberties of the People set out for the Maryland legislature both prohibitions and goals.[11] The most extensive was the Massachusetts Body of Liberties, though it was followed shortly by similar efforts in other colonies, to the south as well as to the north.

Through these codifications and lists of rights, we see the foundation element of self-definition being differentiated into bills of rights. However, the colonists viewed a bill of rights as a virtual celebration of the people's fundamental values. The limitation on government was, as we have seen, that certain actions were not acceptable.

Although the definition of community values was more public and insistent in New England, southerners had their equivalent documents, albeit fewer in number and less dramatic in content. The middle colonies had the example of the others as they came along later, but they also had a strong impetus for developing bills of rights.

William Penn had been the victim in England of an exceptionally unfair and politically motivated trial. Deeply traumatized by the experience, he worked hard to prevent anything similar happening in Pennsylvania. His Charter of Liberties (1682) and the Pennsylvania Frame of Government (1682) reflect a strong and independent concern for rights as we conceive of them today.[12] Certainly Magna Carta was the source of some of his ideas, as well as his belief that he had been treated in a very un-English-like fashion. It is, however, difficult not to see direct experience as decisive in his commitment to fair and equal treatment of all citizens. Penn's ideas in this regard were influential elsewhere

11. "An Act for the Liberties of the People," W. H. Browne *et al.* (eds.), *Proceedings and Acts of the General Assembly of Maryland, Jan., 1637/8–Sept., 1664* (Baltimore, 1883), 75, vol. I of *Archives of Maryland,* 14 vols.

12. These two documents can be found in Thorpe (ed.), *Federal and State Constitutions,* VI, 3047–63.

in the documents of the middle colonies—as, for example, the New York Charter of Liberties and Privileges (1683).[13]

When it finally came time to write state constitutions, Americans frequently distinguished between the bill of rights and the constitution proper. The bill of rights usually came first, as part of or along with the preamble. Then the second section of the document was entitled the constitution, thus leaving open to question whether the bill of rights was part of the constitution. Of equal interest, all but two state bills of rights written before 1789 were effectively written or approved by state legislatures. That had been the practice during the colonial era—again, hardly a way to limit the legislature.

The common law embellished and deepened the American constitutional tradition, but was not its sole source. American constitutionalism is broader, more institutionally oriented, and based upon principles not generally found in Magna Carta or anywhere else in the common law. The principles underlying the colonial documents of political foundation clearly "framed" and logically preceded all but a few borrowings from Magna Carta. This is not to say that English common law had no impact. What Americans thus derived is often what they most cherish in the constitutional tradition. But the common law is only a part in the total pattern of influences on American constitutional design.

One simple way of illustrating the relative influence of common law on American constitutionalism is to consider the pattern of appropriation in the United States Bill of Rights. The ten amendments that form the Bill of Rights contain twenty-seven separate rights. Six of these rights, or about 20 percent, were first stated in Magna Carta. Twenty-one, or about 75 percent, were first found in colonial documents written before the 1689 English Bill of Rights. All but one (the Ninth Amendment) could be found in several of the state constitutions written between 1776 and 1787. When it came to matters of constitutional status, Americans drew most heavily and directly upon their own constitutional tradition, which stretched back through colonial developments. Of the many common law rights that they could have appropriated, Americans were selective. They chose in accordance with their own tradition and did not simply write the common law wholesale into their constitutions.[14]

Saying that English common law had relatively little impact on American constitutional design does not imply a lack of effect on the legal system. English common law was used in all colonies by 1776 as the basis for court procedures, methods of appeal, legal definitions, and other key aspects. Again, however, it

13. The text is in *The Colonial Laws of New York* (4 vols.; New York, 1894), I, 111–16.
14. Stephen L. Schechter, "Constitutional Design and the Adoption of the U.S. Bill of Rights" (Paper delivered at a conference on Constitutionalism: The American and Israeli Experiences, December 21, 1987, Jerusalem).

was selectively appropriated and blended with the colonists' principles and practices.

It is important to distinguish between the impact of common law upon the American legal system and upon American constitutional design. In England the common law was the primary means of limiting governmental power, whereas in America the means was different. The *idea* of limited government does in part derive from it. But in the American constitutional tradition, what *replaced* common law was a new political technique, the written constitution. No matter how important common law was for the operation of the American legal system, the written constitution that framed the system sprang from ideas, principles, and practices evolved primarily in America.

Federalism and the British "Imperial Constitution"

One prominent historian argues persuasively that we must also examine the influence of British constitutional changes on the development of American constitutionalism.[15] Britain went through an extended constitutional crisis that began in the 1630s and was not finally resolved until 1688. Britain's North American colonies spent those years, the first half century of their existence, developing almost complete home rule. The Glorious Revolution found the British Parliament supreme and ready to assert its legitimate control over the colonies. The colonists, however, had come to believe that their local legislatures were each equal to Parliament under the Crown. British constitutional development thus took a giant leap during the seventeenth century, but the form differed at the center of the empire and at its periphery.

The colonists predicated their position on what they viewed as three critical aspects of their charters. First, the king, not Parliament, gave them the charters. Second, they could establish local, elected legislatures. Third, they brought with them the rights of Englishmen, which prominently included the right not to be taxed without their consent. On the other hand, metropolitan Britain underwent a prolonged revolution that ended with clear parliamentary supremacy. The British constitution was permanently altered away from Parliament-under-king to king-in-Parliament, and thus Parliament could regulate any relationship the king might have with the colonies. Ironically, the colonists had to defend the old British constitution if they were to make their attachment to the king worth anything. For almost one hundred years, the center and periphery sparred from their contending positions, until finally the empire foundered on this very issue.

15. Jack P. Greene, *Peripheries and Center: Constitutional Development in the Extended Polities of the British Empire and the United States, 1607–1788* (Athens, Ga., 1986).

Jack Greene argues that for most of the eighteenth century, there were three separate constitutions—one for metropolitan Britain, a set of provincial constitutions for North America and Ireland, and what he calls an "imperial constitution." The imperial constitution was not codified, nor was it even a working understanding. But both sides experienced it as Parliament exercising power over matters of common concern while provincial legislatures dealt with local matters in their respective jurisdictions. Greene argues that being subject to two legislatures was instrumental in habituating Americans to a federal relationship, and thus the colonial center-periphery experience had an important formative effect on American constitutionalism.

Let us place this claim in context. As we have seen, the colonists developed a number of fully codified federal systems, extending all the way to pan-colonial organizations, before 1688. Thus, any experience they had with center-periphery relationships was supplemental, not determinative, especially since local federations were more immediate, more persistent, and more important than were sporadic relations with a distant mother country. Also, the federal lesson supposedly learned from center-periphery relations seemed to have no effect on Irish principles of constitutional design. Finally, the range of powers that Parliament retained in the imperial legislature, and its difficulty bypassing local legislatures to act directly upon the colonists, indicate that the Articles of Confederation comes much closer to the imperial analogue than does the United States Constitution—and the Articles of Confederation was not a federal system, it was confederal.

The Articles lacked a sufficient grant of power to the national government, and the national legislature could not act directly upon the citizens of states. This second characteristic is what made the Articles confederal rather than federal. It could be argued that since the colonists continually insisted Parliament should have little power over the colonies, and since its power should be applied to colonies as corporate entities through the respective legislatures, the center-periphery experience caused the colonists to support not federalism but something similar to what was in the Articles of Confederation. Then we must explain how the Founders moved from the confederal to a federal system.

The essential characteristic of a federal system is a division of powers between two levels of government, each supreme in some areas of policy making. This in turn requires two legislatures, each able to affect citizens *directly*, and something akin to dual citizenship whereby one is a citizen of the nation and of the smaller unit, whether it be called a state, province, or canton. At the Constitutional Convention, the issues most central to federalism were, with one exception, relatively noncontroversial—a point that has received little comment.

The delegates seemed to assume that there would be a division of powers between the national and state governments, and that the powers of the national government would be enhanced. Even the confederal New Jersey Plan contained a significant increase in national powers. When they were finally spelled out, there was surprisingly little opposition to, or even discussion of, this broader grant of power. Nor was there much discussion of having the national government act directly upon citizens of states. The people would elect members of the lower house, and they would therefore act directly upon the citizens. The issue that did create a great dispute, and upon which the convention almost foundered, was the matter of representation in the Senate. Even though federal systems tend to have bicameral national legislatures, an upper house is not strictly needed for a system to be federal.

What a federal system does need for successful operation is some means of resolving conflict between the two levels of government. Usually one is supreme in such circumstances, and there is also some mechanism for protecting the other level against misuse of this supremacy. The U.S. Constitution made one house of the national legislature representative of the states and elected by the states. Thus, the very bicameral body that was supreme also had an internal means for protecting the states over which supremacy was granted.

Many other mechanisms could be used instead, the primary one being the election of the unicameral legislature. Thus, for example, a system of proportional representation could effectively protect state, regional, or other subnational interests. The American states, and the colonies that preceded them, often had legislatures with certain powers and town or county governments with theirs. These federal systems generally combined supremacy at the state level and various means that kept the state legislature (in most cases, essentially unicameral during the colonial era) closely tied to popular consent through elections. Sometimes apportionment in the legislature was tied to the towns or counties; after independence, most states adopted bicameral legislatures, and the upper house frequently was apportioned by counties.

Representation in the Senate was so controversial because it was the one piece in the model that was new. It had no real counterpart in the state or the British political systems, and it was central to balancing the "supreme law of the land" clause. The division of powers between national and state governments, and the provision for dual legislatures and dual citizenship, defined the heart of federalism in the U.S. Constitution. The supremacy clause, coupled with the mode of representation in the Senate, would make the federal system acceptable to both sides.

In sum, most of what was needed to change from a confederal to a federal system did not provoke controversy at the convention. These changes did not depend heavily on relations between colonists and the empire, for then the system would have been confederal, not a federal one. On the other hand, there were federal systems in operation at the state level, though these existed more in the North than in the South.

It is interesting that those who proposed the Virginia Plan were from a state that most resembled Britain in its constitutional patterns. The plan would have essentially imposed a parliamentary system upon America, and the model for nation-state relations would have been similar to the center-periphery system Parliament wanted over the colonies. The New Jersey Plan was proposed by a delegation from a middle state that was among those most inclined toward minimal government intervention of any kind, especially in economics. The New Jersey Plan would have retained a relationship between the states and national government very close to what the colonists had argued for vis-à-vis the British Parliament. The Connecticut Compromise, which produced final consensus on a federal system, was offered by delegates from a state where a federal system was in operation and where the impact of federal theology was strong.

However, some not from New England supported federalism, John Dickinson of Delaware and Pennsylvania being prominent among them. Also, discussion at the convention, to the extent theories were used at all, did not mention a theory of federalism, did not refer to federal theology, and did not address colonial–mother country relations as being in any way paradigmatic. Indeed, the delegates did not even seem to have the word *federalism* to use in their discourse. Although we cannot consider Madison's notes as containing all or even most of what was discussed at the convention, they are complete enough for us to conclude that theory was brought in to defend experience, not as an independent generator of institutional design. Most of what went into the Constitution resulted from reflection upon experience.

To say that men work from their experience is to say that they use the mental habits, perspectives, and exemplars that result either from their own direct experience or from the inheritance of their political culture as expressed in documents, institutions, and practices. Possibly, delegates from the South had more of the "imperial constitution" in their experience, and those from the North had more of federal theology and living under federal colonial and state systems. On balance, however, the decisive fact in the creation of federalism seems to have been the existence of states and state governments that could not be destroyed or rendered meaningless if the Constitution, any constitution, was ratified. An explanation of the choice of federalism rather than confederalism can fruitfully refer to experience in America. There is no reason to deny the relevance of the center-periphery model for colonial and American constitutionalism, but once again this influence is most likely supplemental to other aspects of colonial constitutional development, and not in itself determinative.

Framing American Constitutionalism

We can usefully view the development of American constitutionalism as proceeding within a series of nested frames of influence. The outer frame was defined by the charters that provided for local self-government and the transmission of the common law to America. Within the charter framework, colonists wrote their own foundation documents, legal codes, and bills of rights. Colonial constitutionalism was thus framed by the charters, but the colonists evolved their own tradition that responded more to their own needs and desires than to English precedent. The documents the colonists wrote framed the appropriation of English common law. They did so in the manner and to the extent that common law was in accord with the evolving American constitutional tradition reflected in their own documents of foundation. Thus, portions of Magna Carta were included in many such documents.

The United States Constitution would reflect the consistent but partial appropriation of the common law that became traditional in the colonists' documents. The common law would in turn frame ideas taken from other European sources, whether Commonwealth political theory or Enlightenment thinkers. Since colonial documents of political foundation derived so heavily from covenants and compacts, and thus from the Bible, the general picture would have Montesquieu and Locke framed by Coke and Blackstone, and they in turn framed by the Bible, which was in turn framed by the civil covenants (charters) characteristic of British imperial practices between 1578 and 1725. This general model of theoretical framing will need detailed modification so we can distinguish the three clusters of colonies, but it provides a useful shorthand for sorting out the influences upon American constitutionalism.

The term *frame* or *framing* denotes a shared mental structure that is an underlying support for more complex or differentiated ideas. It not only supports but also delimits later thinking. That is, *frame* here denotes a mental disposition, a habitual inclination, that shapes or directs later thoughts in a certain way or toward a certain purpose. Furthermore, since what is framed rests upon the frame or is defined by it, the frame is like a perceptual ground for figures that otherwise could not be seen.

To say, then, that the charters frame the colonists' documents is to say that without the charters, colonists would not have written their own documents; that the charters defined what was generally possible for them to write; that the charters inclined them to view things a certain way, to consider some things problematic and others not; that the charters provide a meaningful context for what the colonists wrote. The frame does not determine what is framed, but rather delimits it. If the charters had not given as much freedom as they did to construct local government, but instead required each colony to form a military unit run according to a predetermined code of behavior, the content of the colonists' documents would have been much different.

The nature of the colonial documents did not determine how the common law was appropriated, but it did shape the colonists' thinking, direct their attention, and dispose or incline them out of habit to take some things rather than others. In effect, certain parts of the common law had special meaning because covenants, compacts, and charters led the colonists to so endow them. If those documents in turn had not framed the situation the way they did, the colonists would not have been inclined to use English common law at all, or if they had, in an entirely other way.

By the last half of the eighteenth century, the framing had become so coherent and so mutually reinforcing that the colonists could borrow from disparate European thinkers and link what others viewed elsewhere as mutually incompatible ideas. John Locke on natural rights supported both God's will as revealed in the Bible and the traditional guarantees of Magna Carta and the common law.[16] Further, the classical Greek notion of virtue transmitted through Enlightenment authors was seen as congruent with the Christian concept of virtue.[17]

To a great extent the framing narrowed coherently because certain key aspects of the colonists' situation remained the same between 1620 and 1776. They were British subjects with all the inclinations to freedom implied by that status, geographically isolated from direct rule, and left to face threats and opportunities unknown to their peers in England. Every attempt by Britain to bring the colonies closer to central rule foundered upon the facts of geography and colonial perceptions. The colonists were freedom-seeking, but they transformed standard English law and custom into free institutions of a nature and on a scale to that point unknown in human history. The British government was unable to increase control, so generation after generation of colonists could practice the art of making their case for local control of government—what they called liberty.

The arguments that occurred between 1774 and 1776 had been worked out to a great extent in the Stamp Act crisis of the middle 1760s. Those discussions in turn rested upon struggles from earlier years. Constant efforts by colonial legislatures to gain the upper hand over Crown-appointed governors had pro-

16. It is a little-appreciated irony that the primary avenue for the introduction of Locke's thinking into colonial and revolutionary America was through election-day sermons by the clergy. See the pre-1780 sermons reproduced in Charles S. Hyneman and Donald S. Lutz (eds.), *American Political Writing During the Founding Era, 1760–1805* (2 vols.; Indianapolis, 1983).

17. Gordon S. Wood, *The Creation of the American Republic, 1776–1787* (Chapel Hill, 1969), Chap. 1.

duced a capacity for political organization and theoretical argumentation that stood the colonists in good stead in the 1770s. William Penn's struggles against tyranny in the English courts strongly influenced his designs for government in Pennsylvania. Opposition to becoming royal colonies in the late 1600s, recurrent problems with taxes, seemingly endless efforts to get the king or councils in London to ratify colonial institutions and practices—all rested upon the frames of the original charters, the long experience of being essentially self-governing through local legislatures, and the selective appropriation of common law, especially Magna Carta.

These frames led the colonists to use recurrent themes and consistent arguments for almost a century and a half. Those of free British subjects were embodied in documents that Englishmen both in England and in America had written. Over time, because their circumstances and the developing frames of political discourse led the Englishmen in America to move from British constitutional theory toward one of their own, all that remained was for the colonists to finally draw the one decisive conclusion needed for complete independence—by 1774, they were no longer British, but American. The constitutional "revolution" had been evolving for one hundred fifty years. They then had to change how they viewed themselves, and the British were all too ready to help, though unknowingly, in the 1770s.[18]

The historical details of that struggle need not concern us here. We are instead interested in the broad transmission of ideas, practices, and institutions that underlie American constitutionalism. The critical period in this regard begins in 1776. Independence required that the implicit constitutional developments of the colonial era be expressed in working constitutions, first at the state level, and then at the national level. The early state constitutions were the link between colonial and national constitutional development. The Declaration of Independence and the Articles of Confederation were important aspects of the national expression of American constitutionalism. If we are to understand these developments, we must articulate the patterns in American political thinking that flowed through and around the constitutions written between 1776 and 1787.

18. The process of shifting self-perceptions is outlined with precision and in depth by Richard L. Merritt, *Symbols of American Community, 1735–1775* (New Haven, 1966).

6. A Coherent American Theory of Politics

Between 1760 and 1805, Americans wrote many formal, political documents. They also wrote innumerable essays, tracts, newspaper articles, and pamphlets that developed or interpreted the ideas and principles in those documents. The famous *Federalist* papers is one example, as is John Adams' *Thoughts on Government*. However, the outpouring of political writings by Americans during the founding era is far richer in quantity and quality than is generally appreciated.

The discussion here and in the next chapter is based upon a comprehensive examination of Americans' political publications between 1760 and 1805.[1] The approximately one thousand items are representative of the thousands of political tracts, treatises, pamphlets, etc., published during the founding era. Some of the better items will be quoted to convey their "flavor" and tone, and sometimes because it is briefer to quote the original than to reconstruct the argument. One document in particular is cited frequently. *The Essex Result,* published in 1778 in Massachusetts, is one of the finest political tracts written during the era and deserves a broader reading than it now has.

The theory of politics dominant during the founding era was a coherent culmination of one hundred fifty years of political developments in America. The documentary evolution outlined earlier came to fruition in the constitutions of the founding era. Whereas their ancestors had done what they felt necessary and proper without a great deal of theoretical discourse, the need to justify the Revolution and then their forms of government forced Americans to engage in careful, self-conscious political discussion. The cumulative American experi-

1. For the books, tracts, pamphlets, and newspaper articles drawn upon as the basis for this chapter and the next, see the listing of 515 items at the end of Hyneman and Lutz (eds.), *American Political Writing,* 1350–88; the items listed at the end of Herbert J. Storing, "The 'Other' Federalist Papers: A Preliminary Sketch," *Political Science Reviewer,* VI (1976), 215–47; and the items in Storing (ed.), *The Complete Anti-Federalist* (7 vols.; Chicago, 1981).

ence gained considerable depth, coherence, and expansion through the appropriation of ideas from various European sources, but the borrowing was selective, often rather more adaptive than adoptive, and sometimes erroneous.

The Communitarian Context of American Politics

Many Americans have a mental image of the founding era. For example, life then was rude, the population was sparse, the frontier to the west was populated by native Americans and by isolated European families and communities. It is easy to imagine a society composed of highly individualistic people who lived relatively free of government intervention and who most valued freedom from the kinds of social and political restraints under which nations labor today. In fact, the nineteenth century saw the rise of individualism as a dominant American value, and the twentieth century has seen not so much the rise of governmental restraint as the transfer of governmental power and control from the local and state levels to the national level. Americans today are more inclined toward individualism than were people during the founding era, and they would probably find excessive the extent and nature of local and state governmental intervention that earlier prevailed.

The shorthand image of late eighteenth-century America must be rectified if we are to comprehend the colonists' political thinking. For one thing, the vast majority of Americans were, by the 1770s, safe and secure in a town or community. After all, by definition a frontier can hardly contain masses of people. At no time since 1776 has more than 10 percent of the American population lived on what we know as a frontier. Most of the communities then in existence, containing most of the people, had been in existence for a century or more. The frontier was on the other side of the mountains, but life on this side was settled if not sophisticated. Almost every aspect of the economy was subject to regulation of some sort. Morals, the heights of fences, and the right to live in a given community were often subject to local government intervention. Far from valuing complete independence in a virtual state of nature, Americans above all valued the communities in which they lived.

It was as a developing nation of communities rather than of individuals that Americans first formed their constitutions at the state and national levels. They believed that humans develop and maintain their highest moral and material existence on Earth while living in communities. As a working political principle, this conviction was often assumed rather than articulated. Among the many explicit statements was that in 1775 by Samuel Williams:

> We cannot therefore either improve or enjoy ourselves as God designed, but in a state of society. And a state of society will necessarily bring in some constitution and form of government, some general plan and system

of laws; which on the one hand, will point out the office and power of rulers; and on the other, the privileges and duty of subjects.

Williams typically relied on biblical and religious principles. But those writing in a more rationalistic vein and drawing upon Locke began with the same conviction. For example, the following is in *The Essex Result*: "The reason and understanding of mankind, as well as the experience of all ages, confirm the truth of this proposition, that the benefits resulting to individuals from a free government, conduce much more to their happiness, than the retaining of all their natural rights in a state of nature." [2] Locke was widely quoted during the founding era, but American authors typically bent his meaning to fit their own view. The state of nature was not usually portrayed as either a condition of natural innocence or a neutral condition of perfect rights:

> [A]nd view them naked, or clothed in the skins of beasts, exposed to the inclemencies of heat and cold, destitute of permanent dwellings, sometimes starving and at others full, solely depending upon their bow—when we contrast their situation with ours, and behold our fair fields producing a regular supply of bread, as well as helping our flocks to clothe and feed us . . . safe from the storms and cold, and lay down our heads to rest, without any to molest or make us afraid—especially when we consider the blessings and advantages of religion and morality, and the knowledge which by letters is offered to our minds.

The same author then described the problems of governmental regulation, political contention, and social restraint as "those trifling evils which we think we sustain." These authors ask their readers again and again to "reflect on the lonely state of men, without the aid of his fellow men in society, a mere animal of prey in dens and caves." [3] People should consider that "we have many affections which a solitary life would give us little room to exercise or cultivate" and conclude with unerring logic that "[W]e must therefore first of all suppose a real and proper community, or state of civil society, to have taken place." [4] Once

2. Samuel Williams, *A Discourse on the Love of Our Country* (Salem, Mass., December 15, 1775), 9; [Theophilus Parsons], *The Essex Result* (Newburyport, Mass., 1778), 484. The latter pamphlet is reproduced in Charles S. Hyneman and Donald S. Lutz (eds.), *American Political Writing During the Founding Era, 1760–1805* (2 vols.; Indianapolis, 1983), I, 480–522. For an item cited as reprinted, the page number will refer to that reprinting—in this case, page 484 of Hyneman and Lutz. Otherwise, references are to original page numbers.

3. Nestor [pseud.], "To the Publick," in Worcester (Mass.) *Magazine* (December, 1786), 1.

4. Williams, *A Discourse on the Love of Our Country*, 9.

established, such a community allows its members to provide "their mutual assistance towards their own perfection."[5]

During the founding era, the American tendency to see their communities as primarily constituted at the local level was based upon a second principle—that a community has a commonly held set of values, interests, and rights distributed through a limited population. To them it seemed natural that the larger the community in a process of consent giving, the more tenuous the consent. Unless there was sufficient agreement on basic values, interests, and rights, there could be no community. That was true as well for a national community, without which there was no basis for meaningful consent.

Two frequently used words were *liberty* and *consent*. It was an unusual piece of political writing between 1760 and 1805 that did not use both. Civil liberty was the result of consent, and consent was of natural liberty. Because our understanding of these terms has changed significantly, and to a certain extent has been corrupted, let us take a careful look at each.

Liberty, Equality, and Community

For Americans of the eighteenth century, the definition of liberty was positive rather than negative:

> Liberty may be defined in general, as a POWER OF ACTION, or a certain suitableness or preparedness for exertion, and a freedom from force, or hindrance from any external cause; Liberty when predicated of man as a moral agent, and accountable creature, is that suitableness or preparedness to be the subject of volitions, or exercise of will . . . which we find belongeth to all men of common capacity, and who are come to the years of understanding. This liberty is opposed to that want of capacity, by which there is a total ignorance of all moral objects, and so, a natural incapacity of chusing with regard to them.[6]

Liberty meant an independent will, as opposed to any degree of dependency, which was termed "slavery" or "slavishness." In the two-level definition, therefore, *natural liberty* is the state in which everyone is free to act as he thinks fit, subject only to the laws of God; and *civil liberty* is natural liberty restricted by established laws as is expedient or necessary for the good of the community. As we have just seen, since humans reach their highest development in civil society, liberty really means civil liberty. Although there are more restraints in civil

5. Agricola [pseud.], [untitled essay], *Massachusetts Spy* (Boston), October 22, 1772.
6. Levi Hart, *Liberty Described and Recommended: In a Sermon Preached to the Corporation of Freeman in Farmington* (Hartford, 1775), 308, in Hyneman and Lutz (eds.), *American Political Writing*, I, 305–17.

society than in a state of nature, they are chosen. But in a state of nature, restraints are forced upon us by nature and by nature's God. That is why these restraints in civil society are "those trifling evils which we think we sustain." Better to be restrained by laws we choose than by conditions and circumstances over which we have no control—like floods, hunger, and cold. Clearly, then, civil society was freer than a state of nature both because there was more room for choosing conditions and because these conditions would rest upon choice, or consent.

Natural liberty rests upon people's God-given nature, which includes the ability to choose freely. Civil liberty rests upon exercising that God-given ability in order to enlarge men's sphere of choice and to control as much as possible those things affecting their lives. Civil liberty, in other words, rests upon consent. Throughout the period in question, Americans defined political liberty as the people being subject only to laws based upon their own consent. They were not, however, free to consent to laws that were contrary to their natural liberty, *i.e.*, contrary to the laws of God.

> When men form themselves into society, and erect a body politic or State, they are to be considered as one moral whole, which is in possession of the supreme power of the State. This supreme power is composed of the powers of each individual collected together, and VOLUNTARILY parted with by him. No individual, in this case, parts with his unalienable rights, the supreme power therefore cannot control them. Each individual also surrenders the power of controlling his natural alienable rights, ONLY WHEN THE GOOD OF THE WHOLE REQUIRES IT. . . . Let it be thus defined; political liberty is the right every man in the state has, to do whatever is not prohibited by laws, TO WHICH HE HAS GIVEN HIS CONSENT.[7]

We can now state with some precision a third fundamental principle held by the Americans of the founding era. God so created men that regardless of different abilities, all men can give or withhold their consent. Implicit here is an idea of equality that formed a fourth fundamental conviction. Since all civil rights derive from the basic natural right of consent, and since all men have the same capacity for such choice, everyone has the same rights in equal amounts. Theophilus Parsons speaks of God, "who at our births, disperses his favors, not only with a liberal, but with an equal hand." The claim that men possess free will by nature is one that any man can make, and thus men share in this claim equally. This notion did not mean, however, that all were equal in physical, mental, or moral abilities. All men nevertheless had sufficient use of reason, a minimal

7. [Parsons], *The Essex Result,* in Hyneman and Lutz (eds.), *American Political Writing,* I, 487–88.

capacity for free will, and adequate knowledge of the dictates of virtue to be equal in the exercise of their basic liberty—the giving and withholding of consent.

Nor did the doctrine mean that all men could or should be economically equal in the state of nature or in civil society. All can know what is virtuous, but the distribution of virtue is unequal, and some will be willing to work harder or be able to work more effectively. Equality comes at the beginning, in having equal opportunity to display virtue, not at the end, when all might receive the same economic reward regardless of the virtues possessed and used.

The competitive exercise of all the talents in human nature would simultaneously promote the welfare of individuals and the community at large. Indeed, no serious conflict was perceived between individual interests and community interests, as long as individuals did not violate laws of God and nature. Today, however, we are inclined to assume, or hope, that out of many individuals pursuing their respective interests will come the community good. Americans during the founding era began with the good of the community and assumed, or hoped, that individual interests would not lead some astray. If conflict arose between an individual and the community, the former was assumed to be mistaken.

A basic equality of liberty held, regardless of wealth, intelligence, or virtue, so long as one could demonstrate having the minimum requisite for consent giving—an independent will. One way to determine its presence was a property test. During the founding era, if there was a property requirement at all, it was ownership of fifty acres of land or property rentable for forty shillings a year. In America, that excluded surprisingly few white adult males, since land was plentiful and cheap. Those so excluded from voting ranged from 20 percent in parts of New England to 75 percent in Georgia. Overall, and evidence produces conflicting figures, between 35 percent and 50 percent of white adult males failed to meet the property requirement throughout the colonies during the 1780s.

However, while the test was considered appropriate for indicating an independent will, it was not the only test, and it was not slavishly applied. It was the best means for estimating involvement and stake in the community, for showing virtues in the form of industry, frugality, moderation, and practical sense, and for demonstrating a secure financial base so a person could resist bribery and other economic inducements to sell his vote. In some parts of the country it also indicated to Calvinists that a person possessed and practiced moral virtue, since material prosperity and membership in the elect were associated. Sheriffs and local magistrates extended the vote to many who could not pass the property test but who were known to be independent in will, sound in character, and contributing members of the community. In the cities and large towns, anyone paying taxes was usually allowed to vote. Communities generally preferred not to apply the test in such a way as to preclude their judging the merits of an individual case.

The basic point is that upon entering the realm of liberty, one was considered equal to all others in that realm, insofar as liberty was concerned and despite any other inequalities. Of course, since all who gave their consent were equal, the laws consented to should apply equally. Thus, equality under the law derived directly from equality of liberty.

Thus we come to two more fundamental principles of American political thought during the founding era. First, because humans' highest moral and material existence is in communities, and because a community is defined by a commonly held set of values, interests, and rights distributed through a limited population, the people in a community have a common interest in protecting and preserving these values, interests, and rights. Second, when there is a conflict between the values, interests, or rights of the community and those of specific individuals, or a portion of the community, those of the community are superior.

For Americans during the founding era, liberty and equality applied to individuals as individuals in the state of nature. In civil society, however, liberty and equality pertained to individuals as a result of being in a community. For example, a letter to the editor in 1765 began: "As all men spring from the same common Parent, they were all originally equal, and all equally free. Every man had a Right to do what he pleased, provided he did not injure others who had the same Rights as himself." The author then observed that when strength or cunning was used to violate the rights of others, the many had to unite in defense against these violators. He said further: "Hence government arose. By common Consent some were chosen to act for the service of the Rest, and by each individual invested with this power, to render that service effectual. THE SOLE END OF GOVERNMENT WAS THE PUBLIC GOOD." [8] Individuals in civil society give over a matter for public determination only when the good of the whole requires it: community needs take precedence. Otherwise, the matter remains in the private arena.

Instead of viewing the community as antagonistic to individual interests, rights, and liberties, the Americans of that era saw it as the primary means for fulfilling individual goals. The conclusion followed from the first fundamental conviction discussed earlier—humans develop and maintain the highest levels of moral and material existence on Earth while living in communities. As Levi Hart wrote: "Civil society is formed for the good of the whole body of which it is composed. Hence the welfare and prosperity of the society is the COMMON GOOD,

8. "To the Printers," Boston *Gazette,* December 2, 1765, p. 2.

and every individual is to seek and find his happiness in the welfare of the whole, and everything to be transacted in society, is to be regulated by this standard." Another writer said more baldly: "The SOCIAL spirit is the true SELFISH spirit, and men always promote their own interest most, in proportion as they promote that of their neighbors and their country." 9 Furthermore, the communitarian spirit resulted from and enhanced individual equality. "A state of society necessarily implies reciprocal dependence in all its members; and rational government is designed to realize and strengthen this dependence, and to render it, in such sense equal in all ranks, from the supreme magistrate, to the meanest peasant, that each may feel himself bound to seek the good of the whole."10 True self-interest was the pursuit of the common good of the community. Self-interest at odds with the community was mistaken, because it was short term. But the long-run interest of the individual invariably matched that of the entire community.

Although the community's values, interests, and rights were superior to those of the individual or a group of individuals, the community did not have license to ride roughshod over people. Instead, individuals and minorities must place their interests in a broader context on issues that are deemed part of the public arena, *and* government in its treatment of them must refer to long-term community interests and not favor one group of individuals over another. "Common good," "good of the publick," and such phrases are a standard feature of the literature. So are references to "posterity," "future generations," and "generations unborn." The preamble to the U.S. Constitution secured the blessings of liberty to "ourselves and our posterity," echoing that long-term communitarian commitment. The Constitution sets forth a decision-making process designed to produce, as Madison says in *Federalist* 10, "the permanent and aggregate interests of the community." But there must be more than institutions for collective decision-making. There must be values, attitudes, and commitments—a mental stance, if you will—that lead people to frame their discourse, approach problems, and justify solutions in terms of the long-term community interests.

Americans in the late eighteenth century viewed the problem as a double one: how to minimize the effects of factions and then how to make the government serve the will of the community instead of a faction's interests. Ultimately, the people, *as a people*, attempted to govern themselves through their own consent. If we are to believe the newspapers, pamphlets, and public documents,

9. Hart, *Liberty Described and Recommended,* in Hyneman and Lutz (eds.), *American Political Writing,* I, 309; Hamden [pseud.], "On Patriotism," *South Carolina Gazette,* (Charleston), November 29, 1773.

10. Timothy Stone, *Election Sermon* (Hartford, 1792), 842, in Hyneman and Lutz (eds.), *American Political Writing,* II, 839–57.

Americans during the founding era saw themselves as engaged in a common enterprise of some historical importance. As Alexander Hamilton said on the opening page of *Federalist* 1: "It seems . . . to have been reserved to the people of this country, by their conduct and example, to decide the important question, whether societies of men are really capable or not, of establishing good government from reflection and choice, or whether they are forever destined to depend, for their political constitutions, on accident and force." Note that he says "societies of men," not individuals. Americans in the 1780s might have been quite advanced when it came to individual rights, but they understood that they were in their grand experiment in self-government together. One pamphleteer said, "We are traveling together on the same ship."[11]

Liberty and Equality in the Declaration of Independence

Reading the second paragraph of the Declaration by itself, as we tend to do today, leads us to conclude that Jefferson was writing about men as individuals. In a sense he was: Americans of that period believed that individuals in a state of nature were equal in their rights and liberty. But Jefferson was addressing a situation in which civil societies were in a state of nature with respect to each other. Furthermore, in the opening sentence, the document is said to result from a situation in which "it becomes necessary for *one people* to dissolve the Political Bands which have connected them *with another*" (emphasis added). The document was, after all, a declaration of and justification for the colonies' breaking with England, not an abstract essay on individual rights. It was a lengthy list of abuses Americans had suffered as a people at the hands of the English. No one was surprised. Americans had been producing similar lists in their newspapers since the infamous Stamp Act more than ten years earlier. The first of the twenty-eight listed concerns a community problem: "He [the king] has refused to Assent to Laws, the most wholesome and necessary for the public Good." It is not individualism that permeates the list of abuses. Why, then, did Jefferson use the words "all men are created equal"?

The answer is straightforward. As we saw earlier, liberty and equality pertained to individuals in the state of nature, but were focused upon the community in civil society. Furthermore, men have rights and liberty in civil society *precisely because* they were originally free and equal in a state of nature. This fact resulted in civil society resting upon freely given consent. As a consequence, since Americans would be as free as Englishmen in a state of nature, they had the same ability and right to form their own government. Once formed, this self-government was just as valid on either side of the Atlantic. In short,

11. Alexander Hamilton, James Madison, and John Jay, *The Federalist,* ed. Jacob E. Cooke (Cleveland, 1967), 3; "To the Printers," Boston *Gazette,* December 2, 1765, p. 2.

Jefferson was saying that the American people are equal to the English people, because all men are equal in the state of nature and have the same ability to give or withhold consent. His readers knew immediately what he meant.

Since this explanation varies somewhat from the current general understanding, let us examine a few similar statements from literature of the founding era.

From what hath been shewn, it will appear beyond a doubt, that the BRITISH subjects in America, have equal rights with those in BRITAIN.[12]

The ministerial writers, and all the great and little tools on this and the other side of the water, are obliged to confess, that the subjects of America are upon an equal footing with regard to Liberty and Right, with those in Britain.[13]

According to the order of the day . . . this House do UNANIMOUSLY come into the following Resolves.

1. Resolved, That there are certain essential Rights of the BRITISH Constitution of Government which are founded in the law of God and Nature, and are the common rights of Mankind.

2. Resolved, that the Inhabitants of this Province are UNALIENABLY entitled to those essential Rights in common with all Men. . . .

5. Resolved, That His Majesty's Subjects in America, are in Reason and common Sense, entitled to the same extent of Liberty, with His Majesty's Subjects in Britain.[14]

Since men are naturally equal, and their rights and obligations are the same, as equally proceeding from nature, nations composed of men, considered as so many free persons, living together in a state of nature, are naturally equal, and receive from nature the same obligations and rights. Power or weakness does not in this respect produce any differences. A dwarf is as much a man as a giant; a small republic, any body politic having the power of governing itself that has a legislature of its own, is as much a sovereign state as the most powerful kingdom.[15]

From the foregoing number of this paper, it is evident, that every State or body politic . . . is governed by the same fundamental principle, and spirit of law, as a single individual or body natural. It is equally evident that

12. "The Rights of the Colonies Examined," New York *Mercury,* January 28, 1765.

13. "To the Printers," Boston *Gazette,* July 15, 1765.

14. Resolves of the Massachusetts House of Representatives, as printed in Boston *Gazette,* November 4, 1768.

15. Agricola, [untitled essay], *Massachusetts Spy* (Boston), October 22, 1772.

> this colony is to all intents and purposes as free and independent a commonwealth as any federative state, under the general direction of one imperial head as to peace or war, is or can be.[16]

> It is further observed here, that states or communities, as such, have naturally the same liberty which individuals have in the state of nature.[17]

> Separate states—all self-governing communities—stand in the same relation to one another as individuals do when out of society.[18]

> It was not asserted by America that the people OF THE ISLAND OF GREAT BRITAIN were slaves, but that we, though possessed absolutely of the same rights were not admitted to enjoy AN EQUAL DEGREE OF FREEDOM.[19]

Jefferson's words in the Declaration of Independence had added force because they alluded to the then-common formulation that the Americans and the British were individuals in a state of nature. That is, since the king broke the agreement to which the people had consented, the basis for obligation between the two communities was broken. This formulation is also congruent with the American belief that "[W]hen men form themselves into society, and erect a body politic or State, they are to be considered as one moral whole."[20] In this sense, a community can be equivalent to an individual. It is a moral organism standing in a moral relationship to other communities of people. In sum, those reading Jefferson's words would understand that all men have equal liberty to give and withhold consent, that in civil society all men have the same rights while they are members of that society, that any given people have the same right to self-government as do any other people, and that once a people form a government they are on an equal footing with any other self-governing people.

16. The Monitor [pseud.], "No. VI," *Massachusetts Spy* (Boston), January 9, 1772.

17. Simeon Howard, *A Sermon Preached to the Artillery Company in Boston* (Boston, 1773), 189, in Hyneman and Lutz (eds.), *American Political Writing,* I, 185–208.

18. Massachusettensis [Daniel Leonard], "To All Nations of Men," *Massachusetts Spy* (Boston), November 18, 1773, p. 210, in Hyneman and Lutz (eds.), *American Political Writing,* I, 209–16.

19. An American Citizen [pseud.], "On the Federal Government, No. 1," New York *Packet,* October 5, 1787.

20. [Parsons], *The Essex Result,* in Hyneman and Lutz (eds.), *American Political Writing,* I, 487.

7.   Variations on a Theory of Popular Control

Having discussed in detail liberty, equality, consent, and rights, we can address the American theory of popular control of government. It is important to distinguish the major variations on the American theory and to identify the common core of beliefs linking these variations.

The starting place for most American thinking on politics was the idea that the community and its government originate in the consent of the people—a definition of popular sovereignty. Americans during the founding era differentiated between the community and its government, because the latter was supposed to be the creation of the former. In the absence of the distinction, a particular government and the community might be confused and the sense of subservience thereby lost. Many articles and pamphlets drew explicitly upon Locke's notion that the compact creating civil society had two parts or phases— the unanimous agreement to create a society, and then the majority's agreement to create the government. Early colonial documents clearly show that those unanimously signing compacts and covenants had long agreed to be bound thereafter by the majority. The double compact is one of many examples of European ideas borrowed to justify an already long-standing practice in America.

Popular sovereignty rests upon three deeper assumptions that in effect form a unit. Together, they are fundamental to the American form of government. The first is the belief that the American people, if given enough time, can distinguish between what is good (what is congruent with their values, long-term interests, and common rights) and what is not. If the people could not, one would hardly want to include them in the governmental process. And the logically prior assumption is that the American people will choose the good—their own shared values, long-term interests, and rights. Otherwise, there is no point in allowing the people to make the distinction. Once again, *The Essex Result* states the matter clearly.

> But from a single person, or a very small number, we are not to expect that
> political honesty, and upright regard to the interest of the body of the
> people, and the civil rights of each individual, which are essential to a
> good and free constitution. For these qualities we are to go to the body of
> the people. The voice of the people is said to be the voice of God. No man
> will be so hardy and presumptuous, as to affirm the truth of that proposi-
> tion in its fullest extent. But if this is considered as the intent of it, that the
> people have always a disposition to promote their own happiness, and that
> when they have time to be informed and the necessary means of informa-
> tion given them, they will be able to determine upon the necessary mea-
> sures therefore, no man, of a tolerable acquaintance with mankind, will
> deny the truth of it.[1]

The Essex Result goes on to note that because the people at large do not always
have the time or necessary information, the decision-making process must
include a body of men who do have the time and information, who also have
demonstrated that they are virtuous, and who thus can assist the people in their
deliberations.

Elections would filter upward men of greater virtue, on average, than were
found in the electorate. During the founding era, the reasons for this assumption were not far to seek. First, only men well known for their abilities would
come to the attention of the public; second, such men should be actively sought
and supported. Since electioneering was frowned upon, there existed neither
organized campaigning nor grass-roots parties. The men generally available for
election had public reputations, and there was constant discussion in print and
from the pulpit concerning the preferred qualities for legislators. For example,
brilliance without virtue was wasted in a representative. The belief in elections'
elevating virtuous men made the use of representatives, as opposed to the direct
giving and withholding of consent by the people, a viable proposition to begin
with.

The third assumption is implied in the second. If a people can be trusted to
choose the good once it is distinguished from what is not, they must therefore
possess certain qualities that incline them to the good. Logically prior to those
two, and most fundamental to popular government, is the assumption that the
American people are a virtuous people—that they are able and willing to seek
the common good. It could be no other way. If the people are corrupt or lack the
virtues necessary for popular control of government, it would be foolish to ever
speak of popular control, no matter how strong one's belief in free will, the

1. [Theophilus Parsons], *The Essex Result* (Newburyport, Mass., 1778), 489–90, in
Charles S. Hyneman and Donald S. Lutz (eds.), *American Political Writing During the
Founding Era, 1760–1805* (2 vols.; Indianapolis, 1983), I, 480–522.

importance of consent, or the existence of natural rights. The people must be virtuous, or all is for naught.

The community is the primary instrument for eliciting, teaching, nurturing, and protecting the virtue of the people. There is a moral dimension to government, especially to popular government. A passage from a sermon by Phillips Payson is illustrative:

> This religion or spiritual liberty must be accounted the greatest happiness of man, considered in a private capacity. But considering ourselves here as connected in civil society, and members one of another, we must in this view esteem civil liberty as the greatest of all human blessings. This admits of different degrees, nearly proportioned to the morals, capacity, and principles of a people, and the mode of government they adopt; for, like the enjoyment of other blessings, it supposes an aptitude or taste in the possessor. Hence a people formed upon the morals and principles of the gospel are capacitated to enjoy the highest degree of civil liberty, and will really enjoy it, unless prevented by force or fraud. . . . The voice of reason and the voice of God both teach us that the great object or end of government is the public good. Nor is there less certainty in determining that a free and righteous government originates from the people, and is under their direction and control; and therefore, a free, popular model of government—of the republican kind—may be judged the most friendly to the rights and liberties of the people, and the most conducive to the public welfare.[2]

Here is much that is familiar from other political writings by Americans during the era. Linking good government, civil liberty, and public virtue was common at the time.

A major part of the debate between Whigs and Federalists was the extent to which public virtue was sufficient by itself to produce good government. The more radical the Whig, the more decisive was the virtue of the general population. A more traditional Whig was likely to prefer a role for men selected from the population precisely for their demonstrated virtue, not to thwart the will of the people, but to slow down its implementation. More radical Whigs kept the legislature closely tied to the popular will. Traditional Whigs gave it more independence from direct popular control. Theirs was a kind of Burkean search for the common good in which direct response to popular demands might be ill advised.

2. Phillips Payson, *A Sermon* (Boston, 1778), 524, in Hyneman and Lutz (eds.), *American Political Writing,* I, 523–38.

Federalist Variations on Whig Political Theory

The Federalists were even more institutionally oriented: they sought greater protection from majorities and from governmental officials who might attempt to substitute their own wills for that of a deliberative community. The Federalists built upon the assumptions of their Whig predecessors and at the same time raised the theory to new levels of sophistication. Examining with some care the model of government that James Madison worked out in his part of *The Federalist,* we can demonstrate that the assumptions discussed in this chapter are continuous over the founding era, even during the Federalists' great institutional innovations.

In *Federalist* 10 and 47 through 51, James Madison attempted to set forth the theory underlying the design of the basic institutions in the U.S. Constitution. Ultimately, said Madison, Americans sought a stable and effective government that also preserved the liberty they had come to expect. The primary threat to both stability and liberty arose from faction—in particular, a faction of the one, the few, or the many that was tyrannical. Madison's definition of tyranny was the one standard at the time, the *arbitrary* use of power, that is, contrary to the community's permanent, aggregate interests. Thus far he had merely summarized the conventional wisdom inherited from Aristotle, Montesquieu, Locke, and other great thinkers widely read during the founding era.

Madison began to demonstrate the originality of the American constitutional approach when he divided the problem of tyranny into two broad categories, majority tyranny and governmental tyranny (see paper 10 for the former and papers 47 through 51 for the latter). Madison said that the solution to majority tyranny was to eliminate the causes of faction or to control the effects of faction. The first would mean the elimination of liberty, an act obviously contrary to one fundamental purpose of the entire project, or the imposition of the same interests, values, and inclinations, which would be impossible because of human nature.

The strategy for controlling the effects of faction had two parts. The first was to use representation. In direct democracy the majority, almost by definition, would act on a common passion or interest and thus be willing "to sacrifice the weaker party or an obnoxious individual." Democracies, Madison said, were always "spectacles of turbulence and contention," unstable, and threatened the liberties of minorities and individuals. In a republic, on the other hand, an elected group of men "refined" the public views. These representatives "may best discern the true interest of their country" rather than sacrifice it to petty or narrow interests. Representatives were more likely to be wise, patriotic, and lovers of justice.

For Madison's "may" to become "will," there must be an extended republic. If representation is to help avoid majority tyranny, there should be great numbers of citizens in a country of considerable extent. In a small country with a relatively low population, there will be few distinct parties and factions, and the majority on a given issue will likely come from the same party or interest. As a country grows larger and more populous, this likelihood lessens. If the population is large enough, diverse enough, and spread over a large enough area, there will be virtually no possibility that a majority will come from the same party or interest. In an extended republic, that is, there will be no natural majority, and any majority will be a temporary coalition of minorities. There can then be no tyranny because passion has been replaced by the agreement resulting from the bargaining needed to produce a majority.

Two important implications must be noted. First, this is not an argument against majority rule. If Madison and the Founders did not expect the majority to ultimately rule, there would be no need to worry about majority tyranny. Because the majority ultimately will rule, its passions must be spent organizing an extended population and then refined through a small group of men of superior virtue. Second, if the intent is not to prevent majority rule but to slow it down, then the fundamental strategy for controlling the evil effects of faction is *delay*. Make it difficult for a majority to form, and require its expression in an arena dominated by more virtuous men. The two characteristics of successful republican government enumerated by Madison, representation and an extended republic, make delay, or a careful, highly deliberative process, central.

Madison rehearsed the common notion that elections filter upward men of greater virtue. Virtue was present as well in his assumptions. They were logically nested in such a way that all must be accepted if delay, or a highly deliberative process, is a realistic solution to majority tyranny. These three assumptions look familiar.

First, there is little point in delay unless the people and their representatives can thereby distinguish whether a proposed policy serves the community's permanent, aggregate interests. There is little point in assuming that the people can make such a distinction unless one also assumes that preference will then be given to what does serve the community. And the most fundamental assumption is that *the American people are a virtuous people*. With its shared assumptions and convictions, Federalist political theory is a highly sophisticated gloss upon the Whig political theory that earlier dominated American politics. That essential continuity is at the core of American political theory from the founding era.

Madison presented his solution to governmental tyranny in *Federalist* 47 through 51: separation of powers, checks and balances, and federalism. Together they provide a strategy analogous to that for handling majority tyranny. The feared entity, this time government itself, is broken up and dispersed so that one faction can rule in its own interest only with great difficulty. Any faction desiring to control the three branches of government must wait two years for the lower house of Congress, at least four years for the Senate and the executive, and an indeterminate number of years for the Supreme Court. Each has a different constituency: relatively small clusters of citizens scattered across the country in the case of the House, the state legislatures for the Senate, the electoral college for the president, and the president and the Senate in the case of the Court. If one branch is taken over, the others can resist by means of the system of checks. A faction able to gain control of the national government must in effect transform itself into a coalition comprising a clear majority of the population, withstand the test of time induced by delay, and face the deliberative process. Even then, the states' broad powers remain outside the national government's control. The basic solution once again is to fragment and to induce delay.

Madison summarized the solution to majority tyranny with the term *extended republic*. His terms for the solution to governmental tyranny was *compound republic*. In order for the extended republic to work, the country must be large. However, in such a country, the government would become very powerful, itself a source of tyranny, and thus a primary threat to liberty. Size would further prohibit effective government from the national level alone. The compound republic, which we today know as federalism, permits the extension of the republic over an area great enough to prevent majority tyranny. The division of powers that federalism represents also helps to prevent governmental tyranny. The result is elegant and coherent, a considerable advance in theoretical and institutional design. Without federalism, republican government would not have been possible at the national level. Without the belief in a virtuous people, the federal republic would not have been tried.

Virtue, the Deliberative Process, and Majority Rule

What specific virtues did the Americans of the founding era believe they possessed as a people that made them capable of self-government? Overall, they were inclined toward choosing public policies that were for the long-term benefit of the entire community. This relatively simple definition, however, hides a number of complexities and specifics.

American political thought had developed from radical Protestant theology, and thus political virtue had a religious base. The Federalists were trying to ground political thought in the European Enlightenment's transmission of classical Greek and Roman ideas. In this tradition, virtue was the classical Greek sense of *aretē*, that is, being able to do well at a job in the practical realm. For example, if a person was educated, familiar with the rules of justice, fair-minded, skilled in close reasoning, and acquainted with the rights of mankind, he possessed the virtues needed to be a good judge. For at least one brief historical period, encompassing the founding era in America, the moral instruction of radical Protestantism was not in essential conflict with the prudent recommendations derived from Enlightenment political theory.

American political writers of a more classical persuasion frequently noted a connection between morals and prudence: religion and religious education were the primary means of inculcating the desire to pursue the common good. Those writing from a more strictly Christian perspective saw the dictates of reason as simply reinforcing what God commanded in the Bible. As Phillips Payson said, "The voice of reason and the voice of God both teach us that the great object or end of government is the public good."

An interesting aspect of this dual thrust is that religious and secular thinkers could agree on what kind of behavior was essential. For instance, many public documents, including half a dozen state constitutions, listed the following virtues: justice, moderation, temperance, industry, frugality, and honesty. Temperance was the religious equivalent of moderation, a crucial virtue in classical Greece. Industry and frugality might be called essential virtues for a people hoping to achieve national economic independence and develop a strong economy, but American Calvinistic Christians also saw them as religious virtues. Honesty could also serve both traditions of virtue. In Payson's sermon, he lists and discusses as virtues necessary for a free people: love of country, knowledge and learning, a spirit of liberty, the absence of exorbitant wealth, and the relative absence of the lust for power and "other evil passions." [3] Rather interesting from a minister, this list was nevertheless typical, whether the writer was a Whig or a Federalist.

The major factions agreed on the importance of virtue and a deliberative process, but not on the role of virtue and how to ensure deliberation. Radical Whigs pressed for public access to legislative sessions, for example, having newspapers print synopses of the sessions and requiring that each bill be passed by consecutive legislatures, with an election in between, before it became a law. Such provisions provided a great deal of opportunity for community discussion. Traditional Whigs argued for legislatures more independent of short-term majorities, and emphasized a bicameral legislature, methods for identifying virtuous legislators, and procedures that ensured careful consideration—such as multiple readings of a bill. The highly deliberative process for traditional Whigs thus was focused more on the legislature. The Federalists added more institutional mechanisms, among them a system of checks and balances that included the executive.

From their notion of the common good, Americans derived another impor-

3. *Ibid.*, 526.

tant principle: The majority speaks for the community. As it was stated in Berkshire's Grievances:

> Again, in all societies of men united together for mutual aid, support, and defense, there exists one supreme, absolute, and rightful judge over the whole, one who has a right at all times to order, direct, and dispose of the persons, actions and properties of the individuals of the community, so far as the good of the community shall require it; and this judge is no other than the majority of the whole.

Theophilus Parsons explained in *The Essex Result*:

> If a fundamental principle upon which each individual enters into society is, that he shall be bound by no laws but those to which he has consented, he cannot be considered as consenting to any law enacted by a minority; for he parts with the power of controlling his natural rights, only when the good of the whole requires it; and of this there can be but one absolute judge in the State. If the minority can assume the right of judging, there may then be two judges; for however large the minority may be, there must be another body still larger, who have the same claim, if not a better, to the right of absolute determination. If therefore the supreme power should be so modeled and exerted, that a law may be enacted by a minority, the enforcing of that law upon an individual, who is opposed to it, is an act of tyranny.[4]

Writers sometimes added the Lockean proposition that the majority, as the greater force in society, will eventually prevail. Better a peaceful process through majority rule than through violence, which will produce the same result anyway.

Federalists insisted that the majority should be even more deliberative than the Whigs required, reflecting a desire to take into account the potential problem of an intense minority. Given enough time, and a fair deliberative process, such a group might persuade the majority to alter its position, might conclude that intensity was unwarranted, or might reach some accommodation to reduce the powerful differences of opinion. The radical Whigs preferred a more immediate and direct use of majority rule; the Federalists pointed to the problems resulting at the state level from decision-making processes that were tied too closely to simple majority rule. All major factions agreed that the process should be deliberative, but they were divided on how much was necessary and suffi-

4. William Whiting, *An Address to the Inhabitants of Berkshire County, Mass.* (1778), 466, in Hyneman and Lutz (eds.), *American Political Writing*, I, 461–79; [Parsons], *The Essex Result*, in Hyneman and Lutz (eds.), *American Political Writing*, I, 488.

cient to produce decisions that enhanced the good of the entire community. There followed disagreement over the role representatives should play, and thus over the nature of representation in general.

Representation and the Common Good

[handwritten: Majority rule ——> common good]

Despite such differences of opinion, it was generally accepted during the founding era that since the legislature was elected by the majority, it embodied popular consent and thus represented the community. Furthermore, the legislature produced the deliberative sense of the community. How it did so, or should do so, was a matter of controversy.

More traditional Whigs had what today would be termed a Burkean view of the matter. Legislators, men of superior virtue, were elevated by the people to deliberate in a calm, cool manner, detached from factious considerations and seeking the good of the community. Traditional Whigs were inclined to feel that the personal characteristics made little difference, at least insofar as the electorate's respective long-term interests were concerned. Assuming that a population had common values, rights, and interests was the very definition of a community. Once long-run interests were discerned, there was little question but that any citizen, if a legislator, would choose the long-term interest of the people. Thus, traditional Whigs saw nothing inherently unrepresentative in the majority of legislators being wealthy and highly educated. Having legislators with such backgrounds was a positive advantage.

> These qualities [wisdom, firmness, consistency, and perseverance] will most probably be found amongst men of education and fortune. From such men we are able to expect genius cultivated by reading, and all the various advantages and assistances, which art, and a liberal education aided by wealth, can furnish. From these result learning, a thorough knowledge of the interests of their country . . . and an acquaintance with its produce and manufacture, and its exports and imports. All these are necessary to be known in order to determine what is the true interest of any state. . . . From gentlemen whose private affairs compel them to take care of their own household, and deprive them of leisure, these qualifications are not to be generally expected, whatever class of men they are enrolled in.[5]

Theophilus Parsons is here rehearsing the aristocratic principle, not as a definition of the nature of representation, but as a tenet that should underlie a legislature. In effect, the principle constitutes an argument for an upper house with

5. [Parsons], *The Essex Result*, in Hyneman and Lutz (eds.), *American Political Writing*, I, 490.

higher property qualifications so such men would be drawn to the legislative process.

Both the Stamp Act crisis and the outbreak of war with England helped bring to the fore the radical Whigs who pressed for a more direct form of representation.

> The rights of representation should be so equally and impartially distributed that the representatives should have the same views, and interests with the people at large. They should think, feel, and act like them, and in fine, should be an exact miniature of their constituents. They should be, if we may use the expression, the whole body politic with all its property, rights, and privileges reduced to a smaller scale, every part being diminished in just proportion.[6]

Legislators are to be representative of the community by virtue of being made of the same stuff collectively as their constituents. Shared experiences, backgrounds, and values would lead naturally to legislators thinking and feeling like their constituents did. The result would be similar to that of assembling the entire population in the chamber.

There was a third view of representation, one that today seems more familiar. During the founding era, the Federalists spoke vociferously for it. The position had been argued as early as 1765:

> As every distinct interest in a government ought to have its due weight in the administration of publick affairs, so each of those interests should have the appointment of representatives, in number as near as might be proportionate to their interest in and importance to the government in general. Consistency and sameness of interests, ought to be the rule to determine what individuals in a state should vote for representatives for that particular interest.[7]

The author then describes a legislature characterized by competing interests, but one that sacrificed short-term interests to long-term community ones as a result of rational calculation. All major political factions could agree on the crucial importance of a deliberative process and on the legislature's centrality to any such process. The question of adequate or effective representation, however, generated considerable diversity of opinion. In fact, it was the matter of representation that created divisions during the founding era.

6. *Ibid.*, 497.
7. A Freeman [pseud.], [untitled essay], *Georgia Gazette* (Savannah), September 19, 1765.

Bicameralism

The question of appropriate representation arose insistently in discussions of the basis for a bicameral legislature. Some traditional Whigs would have been satisfied with a single house composed of the "better sort" who would calmly and soberly consider the common good. Some radical Whigs would have been satisfied with a single house that accurately mirrored the population and did not embody the aristocratic principle. Two of the early state constitutions did in fact create unicameral legislatures, both on radical Whig premises. However, the overwhelming sentiment was for a bicameral legislature. There are four reasons that are analytically distinct. The simplest argument was that it would enhance the deliberative process. If two houses had to pass legislation, the process would be longer and would engender more care.

A second argument worked from a deeper assumption concerning the nature of power. David Ramsay said in 1789, "[T]he experience of all ages had taught them the danger of lodging all power in one body of men. A second branch of legislature, consisting of a few select persons, under the name of Senate, or council, was therefore constituted." [8] Madison also noted that danger. The creation of a bicameral legislature, he said, especially with an upper house composed of "more virtuous men," seemed one way of dealing with concentrated power in a system in which the legislature tended to be supreme.

A related argument held that there was merit in the notion of a mixed regime. The theory was that the most stable form of government blended the democratic, aristocratic, and monarchic principles. Such a system made use of what was positive in all the major forms of government, and had the added virtue of involving all classes in the decision-making process. The lower house was supposed to embody the democratic principle, the upper house the aristocratic, and the executive the monarchic.

A fourth chain of reasoning began with the general agreement that "[a]ll creatures have not the same capacities; neither are they placed under equal advantages; and, if those be found, whose capacities are equally extensive, still they are different; and seem to be designed for different purposes, and stations, in the great system." [9] Unequal abilities should not lead to political inequality, since political equality rests upon the ability to give and withhold consent, which is shared equally. But they do lead to social and economic inequality, which is similar to saying that there is a "natural aristocracy" based upon ability

8. David Ramsay, *The History of the American Revolution* (2 vols.; Philadelphia, 1789), I, 377.

9. Timothy Stone, *Election Sermon* (Hartford, 1792), in Hyneman and Lutz (eds.), *American Political Writing*, II, 841.

and virtue. Furthermore, there is no inherent, long-term conflict between the interests of wealth in the community and the interests and rights of the people, and both wealth and numbers need to be represented. A bicameral legislature so constructed that one house represents the people and the other represents the wealth of the community would protect the common good better than would a unicameral legislature. *The Essex Result* develops the argument at some length, and it is clear that Theophilus Parsons is speaking about the wealth of the community, not about wealthy persons. Wealth is viewed communally rather than individualistically. What made the Federalists different from other theorists was their tendency to think in terms of wealthy individuals rather than some reified notion of undifferentiated wealth.

The Federalists accepted the four prominent reasons for a bicameral legislature. It would aid the deliberative process, it would avoid putting all power in the same hands, it would increase stability through a mixed regime, and it would protect the common good by representing both the numbers of people and the wealth of the community. The Federalists also added a fifth, representation of the states.

Legislative Supremacy

One of the more significant Federalist innovations was the strategy of using separation of powers and checks and balances to alter somewhat the legislature's preeminence. Having three branches that share the powers necessary to govern is a constitutional strategy so well known that it does not require much discussion here. It is also possible to view the Constitution as establishing mixed government. If the lower house embodies the democratic principle, the upper house the aristocratic, and the executive the monarchic, then separation of powers and checks and balances effectively blend these various principles. However, the standard exposition of the American national government emphasizes these aspects at the expense of one fundamental fact. At the time the Constitution was written, Congress was easily the most powerful of the three branches. Contrary to a common but mistaken understanding of the term *balances,* there was a sharing of powers, but they were not balanced. The two important balances in the Constitution were, first, the different terms of office and, second, the different constituencies for electing people to each branch. The purpose was to make it extremely difficult for any faction to capture all of government and thus concentrate all power in the same hands.

The so-called checks were part of the same system designed to enable the branches of government to block, impede, or slow each other so as to enhance deliberation and to help prevent any faction from getting its way until and unless it controlled all three branches. However, there was no balance with respect to how many checks each branch had, nor was there even a symmetry.

For example, the executive was independent of the legislature insofar as he was elected by the electoral college, which operated at the state level, but once in office he was largely restricted to the veto when it came to checks. Congress, on the other hand, could override the veto, and it also had the power of impeachment. The president as treaty maker required Senate approval; and though he was commander in chief, Congress had the sole power to declare war.

As for the Supreme Court, Congress could alter its size, fix its salary, and determine its appellate jurisdiction. The last check was the most important. Congress could restrict the Court to hearing cases over which it had original, exclusive jurisdiction. Under today's circumstances, that would leave it few cases. In return, the Court had judicial review, but that is not, strictly speaking, a constitutional check. There is no mention of it in the Constitution. Thus, as originally written, the document gave the preponderance of checks to Congress.

In the division of powers, the three most important then were the taxing power, the appropriating power, and the power to declare war. All three rested essentially with Congress. The president could veto, but a determined legislature could override. Even though Congress was clearly predominant, the national executive looked strong from the states' point of view. In those few states in which an executive had any veto power at all, he usually shared it with a council drawn from the legislature.

While the Federalists were highly critical of the kinds of legislation that emanated from state legislatures that were clearly supreme, they did not reject the bases for the nature of representation. The Federalists accepted those but substituted legislative *centrality* for legislative *supremacy*. The legislature was without question the central instrument of government, but the Federalists attempted to make the national legislature a more deliberative body than was the case in state government.

The legislature is the primary deliberating body at all levels of American government, and since the deliberative sense of the community should be the basis for collective decisions, the design of the legislature is critical. One important aspect is size. In pursuit of relatively direct consent and a legislature that mirrored the people, some early state legislatures had been allowed to grow. The result dismayed Whig and Federalist alike. Madison clearly stated what many concluded during the founding era.

> Another general remark to be made is, that the ratio between the representatives and the people, ought not to be the same where the latter are very numerous, as where they are very few. . . . Sixty or seventy men may be more properly trusted with a degree of power than six or seven. But it does not follow, that six or seven hundred would be proportionally a better depository. And if we carry on the supposition to six or seven thousand,

the whole reasoning ought to be reversed. The truth is, that in all cases a certain number at least seems to be necessary to secure the benefits of free consultation and discussion, and to guard against too easy a combination for improper purposes: As on the other hand, the number ought at most be kept within a certain limit, in order to avoid the confusion and intemperance of a multitude.

Madison went on to say in *Federalist* 58 that "in all legislative assemblies, the greater the number composing them may be, the fewer will be the men who will in fact direct their proceedings." Madison was here discussing what Vincent Ostrom calls the "size principle." The extent to which the Federalists built upon earlier Whig political thought can be dramatized by comparing Madison's argument and one Theophilus Parsons made almost ten years earlier.

If the scale to which a body politic is to be reduced, is but a little smaller than the original . . . the number of representatives would be too large for the public good. The expenses of government would be enormous. The body would be too unwieldy to deliberate with candor and coolness. The variety of opinions and oppositions would irritate the passions. Parties would be formed and factions engendered. The members would list under the banners of their respective leaders; address and intrigue would conduct the debates, and the result would tend only to promote the ambition or interest of a particular party. . . . For these reasons, some foreign politicians have laid it down as a rule, that no body of men larger than a hundred would transact business well.[10]

These quotations show how important proper deliberation was to American political thinkers during the founding era, and they indicate the degree to which Federalist and Whig theories overlapped. There was enough commonality linking the various theory-building factions to permit the identification of a core set of assumptions and principles. This came to initial fruition not in the United States Constitution, but in the first state constitutions.

Basic to the American theory of popular control are the following principles: 1) Humans develop and maintain the highest levels of moral and material existence on Earth while living in communities; 2) A community is defined by a commonly held set of values, interests, and rights distributed through a limited population; 3) The community and its government originate in the consent of

10. Alexander Hamilton, James Madison, and John Jay, *The Federalist,* ed. Jacob E. Cooke (Cleveland, 1967), 374, 395; Vincent Ostrom, *The Political Theory of a Compound Republic: Designing the American Experiment* (2nd ed.; Lincoln, Nebr., 1987), 92–101; [Parsons], *The Essex Result,* in Hyneman and Lutz (eds.), *American Political Writing,* I, 498.

the people; 4) All men can give or withhold their consent, a capacity they share equally (regardless of other differences); 5) Since all civil rights derive from the basic right to give or withhold consent, and since all men have the same capacity for such choice, everyone has the same rights in equal amounts; 6) The people in a community have a common interest in protecting and preserving their shared values, interests, and rights; 7) When there is a conflict, the values, interests, and rights of the community are superior to those of an individual or a portion of the community; 8) The majority speaks for the community; 9) The legislature is elected by the majority and therefore represents the community; 10) Government should be based upon, and beholden to, the deliberate sense of the community; 11) The deliberate sense of the community is determined by the legislature, so the legislature should predominate in the government; 12) The primary political virtue is the willingness and ability to seek the common good; 13) Popular elections filter upward men of greater virtue, on average, than are found in the general population; 14) In its deliberations the legislature should seek the long-term common good of the community; 15) In order to effectively seek the common good, the legislature should reflect in its membership all interests within the community in due proportion; 16) Both the wealth of the community and the rights of the community need to be protected; 17) A bicameral legislature is prefereable to one that is unicameral.

The assumptions underlying popular control of government are as follows: If given enough time, the American people can distinguish between what is good (what is congruent with their common values, interests, and rights), and what is not. Second, once the good is distinguished from what is not, the American people will choose the good. And third, the American people are a virtuous people in both the Christian and Greek senses (and thus capable of self-government).

8. The First State Constitutions

Despite the United States Constitution's roots in biblical traditions, classical Greek philosophy, Protestant theology, English common law, English Whig political theory, and the Enlightenment, there was no European precedent or model for it in 1787. Its form and content derived largely from the early state constitutions, as borrowings and as reactions. These often-overlooked documents occupy a critical position in the development of American constitutionalism. They are the culmination of a long process, and the foundation upon which the United States Constitution rests. That is, the Constitution is an incomplete foundation document until and unless the state constitutions are also read.

If we want to know who can vote for members of the House of Representatives, we must look, says Article I, Section 2, at who can vote for members of the lower house in each state, and this requires reading the state constitutions. Senators are elected by the state legislatures. In order to understand the character and composition of these legislatures, we must read the state constitutions. The president is elected by electors whom the states "appoint" in a manner determined by the respective state legislatures. Article IV, Section 2 creates a dual citizenship whereby every American is simultaneously a citizen of the United States and of the state wherein he resides. One result is the existence of a state court system and a national court system. In order to understand the design and operation of the American judiciary, we must, once again, read the state constitutions.

Obviously, the United States Constitution assumes, in fact requires, the existence of state constitutions if it is to make any sense. They are part of the national document and are needed to complete the legal text. The Framers, regardless of their attitude, had no choice but to recognize the brute fact of the existence of state governments. The Framers used the state constitutions because they could not be ignored and because the interweaving overcame their negative effects. Further, the Founders could thereby take advantage of the benefits of federalism.

Complete foundation documents in their own right, the state constitutions each produced political systems that could deal with the collective problems of their respective peoples. Viewed to a certain extent as experiments in self-government, the state constitutions were modified and sometimes replaced in an effort to achieve the goals of effective government and popular liberty. By the summer of 1787, the Framers, many of whom had helped write state constitutions, could draw upon a wealth of experience in the design of institutions and their practical effects. They probably would have been less successful, or not inclined to produce the kind of document they did, had they not previously worked on state constitutions and the Articles of Confederation.

The early state constitutions thus stand as the fulcrum in American constitutional history. On the one hand, they were the culmination of colonial experience and thus embodied and summarized it. On the other hand, they formed the ground for the Articles of Confederation and then for the United States Constitution. The design of the Constitution in 1787 deeply benefited from all the experience at the state level. There are few institutions in the national document, including federalism, that had not been tried out in state or colonial documents. Even more, the state constitutions were virtually part of the national Constitution.

One should not conclude that the state constitutions were the inevitable product of what came before or that the United States Constitution was simply a composite of state documents. The last three decades of the eighteenth century were a time of extraordinary political experimentation and innovation. Between 1776 and 1798 the first sixteen states wrote a total of twenty-nine constitutions, two of which were rejected. The two national constitutions bring the total for the era to thirty-one. The willingness to experiment with new institutions in the service of old, well-established political goals and principles was impressive. Thousands of pamphlets and newspaper articles commented upon the constitutions.

If we accept estimates that in the 1780s about 60 percent of white adult males in America participated in politics at least to the extent of voting, then approximately three hundred thousand persons produced about three constitutions every two years for twenty-two years, and during the same period they wrote at least thirteen hundred pamphlets and newspaper articles a year on political and constitutional matters. In addition, all but one state had annual elections, and there were at least eight thousand elective political positions from president to town surveyor. The numbers suggest a virtual maelstrom of activity for several decades. At the center, and engaging the attention of some thirty thousand politically active men, were the design, operation, and alteration of constitutions, especially at the state level.

How successful were these extensive efforts? Although seven of the first states replaced their initial constitution within ten years or less, the average state constitution written during the era lasted for more than sixty years. One of them, the Massachusetts Constitution of 1780, is the world's oldest constitution. Also, despite the tremendous changes that have occurred in America, today's state constitutions are deeply indebted to and, with only a few exceptions, essentially based upon the models developed between 1776 and 1787. The United States Constitution has survived for two centuries with only twenty-six amendments. Finally, the symbols, principles, and values found in the early state constitutions continue to inform political thinking in late twentieth-century America.

The Colonial Heritage

Let us now begin to set forth precisely what in the early state constitutions resulted from colonial theory and practice. Without a close examination of all the writings by the men involved in drafting the various state constitutions, the following list must be considered provisional and suggestive rather than definitive.

The aspects of the American constitutional tradition that flow from the colonial heritage are:

1. The basics for a civil society are in a single document.
2. The document is replaceable.
3. A double agreement is in the foundation document—first, among the people, with elements from the covenant/compact tradition; second, between the people and the government, with elements derived from charters.
4. The first part of the agreement creates a people and a civil society, and defines the basic goals and values of that society.
5. The first part of the agreement is put in a preamble and/or bill of rights.
6. The second part of the agreement creates a set of institutions for collective decision making.
7. The second part of the agreement is found in a separate section of the document more properly called a constitution.
8. There are certain fundamental beliefs, or basic symbols, upon which constitutional government rests, including:

   a. the belief that humans possess equally the ability to give and withhold consent (the symbols of liberty and equality);

b. the belief that government should be based upon the people's consent (the symbol of popular sovereignty);

c. the belief that the people at large possess those abilities and attitudes required for self-government (the symbol of a virtuous people);

d. the belief that the most important virtue, for the people at large and those in government, is to seek the well-being of the community (the symbols of the common good, majority rule, and deliberative process).

9. There are certain principles of constitutional design, among which are:
   a. frequent elections;
   b. a broadly defined electorate;
   c. legislative supremacy;
   d. limited government;
   e. separation of powers (no holding several offices at the same time);
   f. a system of checks on the executive (and thus the judiciary), primarily through the power of the purse;
   g. division of power between colonywide and local legislatures, often in a federal structure.

10. Certain rights are inalienable, including:
   a. the right to give and withhold consent;
   b. the right to freedom of conscience;
   c. the right to a trial by a jury of one's peers.

11. All other rights are alienable when the common good so requires and when the people or their representatives consent.

12. These alienable and inalienable rights are listed in a bill of rights.

All those aspects came to Americans in 1776 through the three frames of charter, covenant, and common law. However, some important points of American constitutionalism remained to be worked out, partly in the early state constitutions and partly by the Federalists in the national Constitution. For example, separation of powers was not a new idea, but a theory with practical institutional consequences was not yet fully articulated. Neither bicameralism nor an independent executive was yet part of American political thought. The idea of electing a special convention to write a constitution, which the people would then approve in a referendum, was not yet well developed—these were more often than not legislative activities. Also, the concept of using an amendment process, as opposed to replacing the entire document, did not yet exist.

The early state constitutions contributed significantly to the development of each of these constitutional principles, though some reached final fruition only in the national Constitution of 1787. For example, the distinction between normal legislation and extraordinary political acts such as the design and approval of constitutions was only partial in 1776. Certain state constitutions, such as the

1780 Massachusetts and 1784 New Hampshire documents, would fully articulate and exemplify the distinction, and the Federalists would ratify the principle. The idea of checks and balances was present institutionally in the early state constitutions, but it was up to the Federalists to articulate the theoretical underpinnings. By 1776, American constitutionalism was well developed. The early state constitutions would significantly advance that stage, which would be apparently completed in 1787. But, as we will see, American constitutionalism continued to evolve.

American patriots of the 1770s frequently referred to themselves as Whigs, a symbolic bow to the commonwealthmen of the previous century with whom they shared much and who also called themselves Whigs. Some have concluded that the similarity in beliefs as well as in name indicates that the commonwealthmen's theory was the decisive influence on the American constitutional tradition. The English writers of that period certainly swayed the Americans, but once again the colonists' selective appropriation deepened and made more precise their view of politics. Furthermore, the English Whigs had been relatively short-lived. By the 1730s, they were politically defeated, in theoretical disarray, and in the process of evolving into something else. On the other hand, in America the essential Whig approach to politics predated the Commonwealth, developed largely independent of political events in England between 1640 and 1660, continued to evolve and dominate American politics for the next half century, and heavily influenced American politics well into the twentieth century. Of greater concern to us, the Whig political principles, assumptions, and commitments inherited from the colonial era dominated the literature surrounding the writing of the first two dozen state constitutions, and thereby formed the basis for the constitutions themselves.

In late 1775 the Continental Congress instructed the states to draft constitutions that would "establish some form of government" independent of the Crown. Three states chose to continue under their respective colonial charters. The Massachusetts Explanatory Charter (1725) modified the Massachusetts Charter of 1691 to bring it more in line with the practices originally evolved through such documents as the Pilgrim Code of Law (1636), the Massachusetts Body of Liberties (1641), and the Puritan Laws and Liberties (1658). The Connecticut Charter of 1662 basically confirmed the Fundamental Orders of Connecticut (1639) as the operative constitution in the combined Connecticut and New Haven colonies. The Rhode Island Charter of 1663 confirmed the government that had evolved from the compacts forming the four original settlements through the Plantation Covenant at Providence (1640), the Government of Rhode Island (1641), and the Acts and Orders of 1647. Massachusetts, Rhode Island, and Connecticut continued to operate under constitutions written during the previous century.

The First Newly Written State Constitution

New Hampshire wrote the first new constitution framed by an independent American commonwealth. The document is only eighty-eight lines long.

> Voted, That this Congress takes up CIVIL GOVERNMENT for this colony in manner and form following, viz.
>
> WE, the members of the Congress of New Hampshire, chosen and appointed by the free suffrages of the people of said colony, and authorized and empowered by them to meet together, and use such means and pursue such measures as we should judge best for the public good; and in particular to establish some form of government, provided that measure should be recommended by the Continental Congress: And a recommendation to that purpose having been transmitted to us from the said Congress: Have taken into our serious consideration the unhappy circumstances into which this colony is involved by means of many grevous and oppressive acts of the British Parliament, depriving us of our natural and constitutional rights and privileges. [There follows a list of grievances.]
>
> The sudden and abrupt departure of his excellency John Wentworth, Esq., our late Governor, and several of the Council, leaving us destitute of legislation, and no executive courts being open to punish criminal offenders; whereby the lives and properties of the honest people of this colony are liable to the machinations and evil designs of wicked men, THEREFORE, for the preservation of peace and good order, and for the security of the lives and properties of the inhabitants of this colony, we conceive ourselves reduced to the necessity of establishing A FORM OF GOVERNMENT to continue during the present unhappy and unnatural contest with Great Britain; PROTESTING and DECLARING that we neaver sought to throw off our dependence upon Great Britain, but felt ourselves happy under her protection, while we could enjoy our constitutional rights and privileges.[1]

In this constitution, a single document, the people of New Hampshire grant Congress the power to make laws and write a new constitution. The relationship is asymmetrical, for the people have ultimate power. Those in government are to preserve peace and good order and protect lives and property, all according to the procedure set forth in the second part of the document. The constitutional elements derived from charters are present.

As for the foundation elements from covenants, there is a carefully wrought

1. The text is in Francis N. Thorpe (ed.), *The Federal and State Constitutions, Colonial Charters, and Other Organic Laws of the United States* (7 vols.; Washington, D.C., 1907), V, 2451–53.

explanation for why the document is needed. A people is assumed already to exist from colonial times, and therefore none is created here. The Lockean notion of one agreement creating a people and another creating the government is implicit here (though, as we have seen, the idea predates Locke in America). The assumption of a preexisting people strengthens the sense of continuity with the colonial era. The document creates a civil society, here called a "form of government." The self-definition is attenuated—there is no bill of rights. We do see a people seeking peace, order, justice, and security. Most of the document describes political institutions. The prominence of this last foundation element is typical of an American constitution in evolved form, but the document also derives from the covenant/compact tradition.

Herein also are the basic symbols first encountered in the early colonial documents. They see themselves as a virtuous people (at least as an "honest people"), and they speak of pursuing the common good. Government obviously rests upon the consent of the people, and popular sovereignty necessarily implies a free people as well. There is a commitment to equality: apportionment of the upper house is based on distribution of population, and property requirements for voting and for holding office are relatively few.

Aside from popular sovereignty, there are many other principles of constitutional design. The use of elections implies majority rule, though that is nowhere explicit. The bicameral legislature, the provision that all laws must be passed by both houses, and the careful description of the logic used to reach the point of writing a new constitution, all indicate a commitment to a deliberative process. A representative body is kept close to the people through annual elections. The lower house selects the upper house, or council, the first time, but thereafter the people do. The document thus reflects a minimal commitment to the principle of filtering upward men of greater virtue. Similarly, there are no property requirements for voting, and a freehold is required for holding office in the upper house only. The same evidence also points to the principle of limiting the electorate to those of independent will and with a stake in the community. Other legislation required a poll tax for voting, but that was not extreme for the time.

The legislature has supremacy: it makes all laws and elects or appoints all officers. Aside from the reference to the rights and privileges of Englishmen, which brings in the common law, there is no explicit reference to rights. The people's basic right to consent to taxation and to government is clearly implied in the language of the document. There is no mention of local control beyond having each county elect its respective members of the upper house in the future.

In sum, New Hampshire wrote a rather radically egalitarian version of an American Whig constitution. The majority, through its legislature, had relatively few restrictions on its power, except in the adherence to a process of decision making and in the limits implied in the common law.

The Next Two Constitutions—The South

The New Hampshire document was adopted in January, 1776. In March, South Carolina adopted the second new constitution. Its long introduction details abuses by king and Parliament similar to the list to be published in the Declaration of Independence four months later. The charter elements, compact elements, and basic symbols found in the New Hampshire Constitution are generally in the South Carolina document as well. The latter is somewhat more traditionally Whig in its principles of constitutional design.

The lower house elects the upper house, and together they elect the governor and his privy council. Two different sections require a separation of the executive branch from the legislative through a prohibition of holding several offices at once. Legislative supremacy is limited only by an executive veto, but then the executive, a creature of the legislature, could hardly be expected to have an independent will. The legislature is apportioned according to the population of counties. Electors have to have at least fifty acres freehold. Property requirements for officeholders are about the same as in New Hampshire, but the governor must be worth at least £10,000. South Carolina's attachment to the principle of filtering upward men of greater virtue is clear.

Otherwise, there is the general commitment to popular sovereignty, majority rule, deliberative processes, and representation. Elections are to be every two years. Only this document and the 1790 South Carolina Constitution—out of the first twenty-five state constitutions—do not call for annual elections. There is no bill of rights in the 1776 constitution, nor is there any mention of common law rights beyond a section guaranteeing jury trials.

Three months later, in June, 1776, Virginia adopted its constitution. The principles underlying its design were similar to those of South Carolina, though it was somewhat closer to what would become the main Whig form. Both houses were elected by the people, and the legislature elected the executive. As in South Carolina, the legislature appointed members to the courts. No property requirements were specified for voting, and the requirements for officeholders were minimal—a freehold, usually of about fifty acres.

The discussion of individual documents could continue at great length. It will, however, be more fruitful to look at all the early state constitutions.

An Overview

It is useful to divide eighteenth-century state constitutions into three "waves" of adoption. The first followed quickly after the Continental Congress in May,

1776, recommended that the states build new governments. The second included three constitutions that resulted from longer deliberations and three that replaced earlier documents. The third wave will not concern us here. It includes constitutions by three new states and seven states' reconsiderations of their constitutions in light of Federalist political principles.[2]

	First Wave		Second Wave		Third Wave
1776	New Hampshire	1777	New York	1789	Georgia
	South Carolina		Vermont	1790	South Carolina
	Virginia	1778	South Carolina		Pennsylvania
	New Jersey	1780	Massachusetts	1792	Delaware
	Maryland	1784	New Hampshire		Kentucky
	Delaware	1786	Vermont		New Hampshire
	Rhode Island			1793	Vermont
	Connecticut			1796	Tennessee
	Pennsylvania			1798	Georgia
	North Carolina				
1777	Georgia				

Each of these constitutions defines a political system (institutions for reaching collective decisions) and a political culture (the values that inform and animate the system). What is striking is that the documents display considerable inventiveness, but there are nevertheless strong institutional similarities and a political culture, with three variations, basic to them all.

The first eighteen state constitutions contain the following institutions: 1) A bicameral legislature (sixteen constitutions. Pennsylvania, not in 1776 but in 1790; Georgia); 2) Direct popular election of the lower house; 3) Enfranchisement of white adult males (eight to ten times above what it was in England); 4) Direct popular election of the Senate, usually the same electorate for both houses (seventeen constitutions. Maryland elected an electoral college, which in turn elected the Senate); 5) Annual elections for the lower house (not South Carolina in 1776); 6) Annual elections for the Senate (ten constitutions), and three had staggered, multiyear terms; 7) Legislature elects the executive (nine constitutions), or a popular election essentially identifies the major candidates from among whom the legislature picked the governor (six constitutions); 8) Annual elections of the governor (fourteen constitutions), biennial elections (two constitutions), and triennial elections (two constitutions); 9) Voters had to own property, usually about fifty acres or the equivalent (twelve constitutions),

2. Although not admitted as a state until 1791, Vermont had already written and adopted two constitutions. Therefore, the 1793 document is its first true state constitution, but its third adopted one, and thus simultaneously a reconsideration of its earlier efforts.

or had to be taxpayers (four constitutions). Two had no property requirement; 10) There was the same property requirement for voters electing the upper house and the lower house (thirteen constitutions); 11) There was the same property requirement for voters electing the executive and the lower house (eight constitutions); 12) Ownership of property necessary to run for the legislature (sixteen constitutions), with few exceptions requiring more property to run for office than to vote; 13) More property required of those running for the upper house than for the lower house (ten constitutions), and usually even more property was required of those seeking the governorship; 14) Bills of rights (except for Massachusetts, Connecticut, and Rhode Island, which initially operated as states under colonial charters, and New Hampshire and South Carolina, which wrote constitutions before the Declaration of Independence); 15) Alienable rights, with only two consistent exceptions—the right to free exercise of religion and the right to trial by jury; 16) State legislatures wrote the documents (thirteen constitutions), usually after an election during which it was made clear that the new legislature would also write a new constitution. The constitutions of Massachusetts (1780) and New Hampshire (1784) were written by a convention elected solely for that purpose *and* submitted to the people for ratification; 17) Amendment process (four constitutions in the first wave), in two of those instances the legislature is the amending agent. During the second wave, an amendment process is more frequently mentioned, but except for Massachusetts and New Hampshire (which give the amendment power to the people), the power is invariably given to the legislature.

Far from exhausting the similarities, the list allows us to outline the essential form of government that the early state constitutions produced. Perhaps most obvious is the manner in which the political systems had a bicameral legislature that was supreme. The executive, usually chosen by the legislature, was invariably weak. Courts were directly under the legislature, whereas in colonial times they had been under the executive.

This strong inclination to legislative supremacy is not surprising. The locus of colonial politics was the perennial struggle between the Crown-appointed governor and the locally elected legislature. Using broadly based suffrage, the colonists kept tight control of legislatures, which gradually gained more power in most colonies. The relationship was so close that when the colonists spoke of "the government," they usually referred to the executive only. The legislature was their protector against governmental tyranny, and they saw it as much more effective than were bills of rights and courts.

With the coming of independence, Americans naturally retained their preferences for the legislature. The executive branch, though recognized as performing necessary functions, was stripped of power and made dependent upon the legislature. Typical provisions in state constitutions, in addition to having the legislature elect the executive, required legislative approval for executive appointments; refused the executive veto power; often created a small group of legislators to assist the governor in approving legislation or granting pardons and generally tell him what to do; and, of course, moved the courts from the executive to the legislative branch. In second-wave documents, as compared to those of the first wave, the executive recovered somewhat from his position of virtual political servitude. The first tentative steps were taken in the New York Constitution of 1777, and the 1780 Massachusetts document describes a resurrected executive. By 1787, only four states had executives worthy of the name.

Legislative supremacy, direct election of both houses, annual elections for all offices including governor, property requirements for voting, the same property requirements to vote for all offices, and above all a broadly defined electorate were among the many manifestations of a general commitment to government based on popular consent. If we exclude legislative supremacy, the list also represents the means, along with other devices, whereby the powerful legislatures were kept close to the people and made highly responsive to popular majorities.

Linking voting rights and property ownership does not seem to belong on any list of instruments for government by consent or for keeping the legislature close to the people, yet it does. There were essentially four arguments for property qualifications: owning property gives a person an independent will; property gives a person a stake in the community and thus ties the owner to its well-being; anyone who levies taxes must also be subject to them; and the use of property should be subject to the majority decisions of property owners only.[3] Despite such requirements, the states produced the broadest electorate in the history of the world up to that time. The major problem with state constitutions was not that such qualifications limited the electorate. Instead, the electorate was so closely tied to a supreme legislature, the constitutional system was unbalanced. Americans brought with them to independence only a portion of the successful constitutional system to which they had belonged as colonists. There was an inevitable period of adjustment during which political institutions lagged behind political needs. It is worth contrasting the operation of the colonial system and the one in effect shortly after independence.

The colonial American view of majority rule involved consensual decisions. Given the highly homogeneous populations of most colonies, this is not unexpected. The most important issue on which there was no such decision was Christian sectarianism. The colonists removed sectarian considerations from

3. See Willi Paul Adams, *The First American Constitutions* (Chapel Hill, 1980), 208–17; and Donald S. Lutz, *Popular Consent and Popular Control: Whig Political Theory in the Early State Constitutions* (Baton Rouge, 1980), Chap. 4.

politics, though they continued to inject broadly Christian values into constitutions.

Although there was no true aristocracy in America, colonial legislatures were nonetheless dominated by wealthy, educated men. Their higher standards of civility and more pronounced preference for stability and order, in addition to the striving for communitarianism over factionalism, created a situation in which highly democratic legislatures operated largely free of what are usually viewed as the natural excesses of democracy. Nor did it hurt that a governor, usually appointed by the Crown, stood as a barrier to unbridled majoritarianism.

Independence rapidly altered circumstances. With only a few exceptions, most notably in Connecticut and Rhode Island, the governors as barriers disappeared, and in their place were anemic executives. The politics of deference seemed to vanish almost overnight, in part because of the rhetorical and theoretical stance necessitated by the opposition to Britain. Also, about a third of the "better sort" were Tories and were abruptly forced out of American politics. In many cases the colonial legislatures contained enough of these British sympathizers, so that alternate legislatures were elected in a successful attempt to bypass Tory efforts at moderation. In the operating state legislatures, and in those created by the new constitutions, the presence of the "better sort" declined sharply from majorities as high as 80 to 85 percent to minorities. They were replaced by moderately well off citizens, often similar to the yeoman farmer that Jefferson seemed to prefer.[4] There was also a drastic decline in the number of lawyers sitting in legislatures. Finally, the electorate increased as suffrage requirements were relaxed somewhat or simply not enforced as rigorously. In most states the electorate probably expanded by 10 to 15 percent. However, since the Tories were usually disenfranchised, and they represented 10 to 15 percent of those who voted regularly, the net change was not so much an expansion in the electorate as a redistribution in the economic classes now voting.

In effect, the situation was not really much more democratic than it had been before independence. However, the circumstances were significantly altered. The governors were now missing. Not only had they helped restrain legislative excess, they had also effectively provided a common enemy for the many colonial factions who papered over their differences to do political battle. With the common enemy gone, factionalism seemed suddenly to worsen. There were many more voters from lower socioeconomic levels who replaced the now-excluded Tories. This electorate used the available democratic means and the

4. Jackson Turner Main, "Government by the People: The American Revolution and the Democratization of the Legislatures," *William and Mary Quarterly,* 3rd ser., XXIII (1966), 391–407.

institutions from their colonial past to press demands upon legislatures that now lacked most of the experienced, legally trained members of previous years. The balances resulting from the system of deference were gone with the changes in legislative membership and the revolutionary rhetorical style. An artificial yet useful communitarian consensus on monetary matters had existed among legislators before independence, but that did not survive. In its place was economic and social factionalism, a more accurate reflection of the divisions within society. In sum, it was a classic case of political culture lagging in the face of rapid change. The constitutional system was out of balance—part of the old system had been kept but another part lost. A new constitutional *system* was needed.

A New Constitutional System

There were efforts to keep as much of the old system as possible while replacing its lost or obsolescent portions with new institutions that made sense in the permanently altered circumstances. The process began not with the Federalists, but with those framing state constitutions. The second wave of constitutions reflects experimentation in this regard. By 1787, four states had revised their initial documents in ways that kept the strong legislatures closely tied to the population, but introduced new restraints. A somewhat stronger executive, stronger bills of rights, and attempts to distinguish between normal legislation and the writing and amending of constitutions are examples of this trend at the state level. It is notable that Connecticut and Rhode Island functioned without revising their constitutions. Their governors had for many years been subject to popular election, and the balances in their constitutional systems had already been worked out and could be retained intact.

The Federalists can be called conservative in one respect. They worked hard to replace some of the more radical state constitutions, especially the Pennsylvania document of 1776. As a result of their efforts, the new constitutional system preserved, perhaps conserved, what remained of the prewar system that was still of value. For example, Federalist concern over majority tyranny makes sense only if they intended to retain ultimate majority rule. They were not antimajoritarian but were seeking ways to restore balance to the system. Another example is the Pennsylvania Constitution of 1790, which the local Federalists wrote to replace the radical 1776 document. There is in it no real retreat from ultimate majority rule. A senate was added and had four-year staggered terms. The governor had a three-year term instead of one year, and he was also given some significant power. But both branches of the legislature and the governor were to be elected directly by the people, there was no property requirement for those running for any office, and there was no property requirement for voters. Thus Pennsylvania had the broadest electorate of any state, virtually universal manhood suffrage. The Federalists did this, knowing full well that that very electorate would elect Pennsylvania's members of the House of Representatives and a state legislature that would vote on the state's two senators.

The United States Constitution is usually viewed as conservative or reactionary because the president and the Senate are not elected directly by the people. These devices are for filtering and slowing down the majority, not for replacing majority rule. The members of the electoral college are elected by the states and meet in their respective states. Those engaged in an antimajority cabal would more likely have used the Senate to elect the executive, or at least brought the electors together in one place where their deliberations could be better controlled. Another little-noted aspect is that under the Articles of Confederation, Congress was elected by the state legislatures; in the U.S. Constitution, however, the lower house of Congress is elected directly by the people. If the Federalists were bent only on removing government from the people, this hardly seems the way to do it.

Nor is this all window dressing for a power grab by nonmajoritarians. The three most important powers of government, to tax, to appropriate, and to declare war, belong to Congress, and the two houses of Congress represent a direct majority of the people and the state legislatures closely tied to state majorities. The president has veto power and the powers of appointment and treaty making, but the first is subject to congressional override and the other two require Senate approval. Certainly this is a resuscitated executive, but the system of checks and balances in the U.S. Constitution greatly favored Congress and reflected a preference for legislative predominance.

One lesson learned from the earlier state documents was to take the judiciary away from the legislature. Putting the national courts under the executive would have been a conservative response, but instead the judiciary became a separate branch. This salutary innovation, one of America's major contributions to constitutional history, was copied later at the state level and by many nations around the world. A separate judiciary helps to weaken the legislature compared to state legislatures. This is one of the clear instances in which the United States Constitution is in reaction to negative aspects of the state documents.

The Constitution is not a reactionary document. It is forward looking, it successfully created a new constitutional system appropriate to new political circumstances, it conserved what was best and central in the earlier American constitutional tradition, and it built upon and in many important respects derived from state constitutions. It is not useful to imply that the Constitution is primarily a reaction to the evils perpetrated by fundamentally flawed state constitutions. Most state constitutions were retained intact for many years after 1787. When finally revised significantly or replaced, they became even more democratic than they had been. This is hardly evidence that excessive democracy had been their primary flaw. And from 1787 onward, the state constitutions were an integral part of the national Constitution.

The commitment to popular control of government continued at both the national and state levels. It was extended at the national level by means of perhaps the most revolutionary idea to come out of the founding era—an amending process contained in the Constitution itself. Any attempt to characterize the United States Constitution as simply conservative is likely to be misleading, unless one asks what it was supposed to conserve. It preserved the American constitutional tradition, which stretched back into the colonial experience and of which the Constitution is the ultimate expression. It preserved the basic commitments, values, and institutions of the early state constitutions. The United States Constitution is best described as creating a federal republic, and both federalism and republicanism are legacies from the early state constitutions.

9.   The Declaration of Independence

During the colonial years, Americans had evolved the practice of using a compact to organize themselves as a people, to create a government, to set forth their basic values, and to describe the institutions for collective decision making. By linking the last foundation element to the charter form, Americans created from the compact and the charter a new type of political document, which we now tend to call a constitution. However, during the last half of the eighteenth century, the term *constitution* referred primarily to that part of the foundation document containing the institutional description. The entire document, with all the foundation elements, was a compact.

The differentiation of a complete foundation document into two parts—one composed of a preamble and a bill of rights, the other describing the form of government—had a number of interesting and useful implications. For example, John Locke saw civil society as arising from a double agreement—the first a unanimous agreement to form a society and be bound by the majority in collective decisions, and the second a majority agreement on the form of government to have. The great strength of such a view was that the majority could alter or overthrow the government without forcing the people back into a state of nature. Since the first part of the agreement was still in effect, and was self-executing, the majority would quickly build a new government. Replacing a government thereby became a riskless and relatively easy thing to do. The idea was not original with Locke, however; it was in earlier writings by Europeans and was implicit in many colonial documents. Indeed, the earliest political covenants often used unanimous consent, an important aspect of which was the agreement to be bound by the majority in designing government and passing laws.

Americans could likewise create themselves as a people and set forth their basic values and commitments in one part of a document, the preamble and bill of rights, with the expectation that changing the second part, which described the form of government, would not alter or endanger the first part. A distinction between a constitution and a bill of rights thus made sense from Locke's point of view, since the majority could easily and safely revise or replace a constitution and thus a form of government. It also made sense for Americans, since that is what they had been doing since long before Locke published his *Second Treatise*.

Separating the two parts of a compact in principle also meant they could be separated in fact. That is, the bill of rights and/or the document standing as a social compact could be approved independently and kept safe from any tampering while a constitution was being modified. For example, on the same day in 1776, Delaware passed its Declaration of Rights and its constitution but published them separately, even though the last article of the constitution (Article 30) states that neither the Declaration of Rights nor five sections of the constitution could be violated. Clearly, the two pieces, though separate, were firmly linked. In one way or another, all the first fourteen states except Georgia made the distinction by separating their documents into two parts or through other explicit means. The preamble to the New Jersey Constitution of 1776, for example, described itself as a compact composed of a "charter of rights and the form of a Constitution."[1]

Colonial Americans preferred as foundation documents compacts that contained constitutions. After independence, Americans used the same form to establish their state governments. It would be surprising if their national document was not similar. The Declaration of Independence together with the first national constitution, the Articles of Confederation, were the Americans' national compact. When the Articles proved inadequate, the Constitution was written in the summer of 1787. There was, however, no need to replace the Declaration of Independence, since the people it created still existed. Changing the government but leaving the social compact untouched was in line not only with Locke's theory but also with long-standing practice in America. If the social compact represented by the Declaration of Independence had not still been in effect, there would have been no basis for a new national constitution. Americans, then, still live under a national compact.

The Declaration of Independence and the preamble to the U.S. Constitution together create a people, define the kind of people they are or wish to become, and establish a government. The Constitution describes the institutions for collective decision making. Few Americans think about the documents in this fashion, at least in an explicit way, yet few seem to find it strange that the

1. The Declaration of Rights is recorded in *Laws of the State of Delaware, 1770–1797* (2 vols.; Newcastle, 1797), II, 89–102; New Jersey's constitution is in Francis N. Thorpe (ed.), *The Federal and State Constitutions, Colonial Charters, and Other Organic Laws of the United States* (7 vols.; Washington, D.C., 1907), V, 2594.

Bicentennial lasted from 1976 through 1987. Americans understand the connection between the Declaration and the Constitution almost intuitively.

The Declaration's Pedigree

The Declaration of Independence was not written in an intellectual vacuum. Nor did it suddenly spring from the minds of one or a few men. First of all, fundamental truths are not suddenly discovered in such impressive quantity and with such clarity or assurance. Thomas Jefferson wrote to Henry Lee on May 8, 1825, about the sources of the Declaration: "Neither aiming at originality of principles or sentiments, nor yet copied from any particular and previous writing, it was intended to be an expression of the American Mind." In the same letter Jefferson says that the ideas come from a variety of sources, and that the Declaration benefits from the writings of all the great writers on liberty— "Aristotle, Cicero, Locke, Sidney, etc."[2] Jefferson is signaling the extent to which the Declaration is an analytic assimilation of American political ideas derived in part from some of the great minds of the past. There is too much here—one or a few men cannot take credit for it all.

Also, most of the Declaration of Independence, in its ideational content and its wording, can be traced to earlier documents written by Americans. As we saw in Chapter 6, the phrase "all men are created equal" was essentially the repetition of a widely employed formula. If Jefferson had meant something different, and the vast majority of people took the phrase in some other sense, then the compact was most unusual. Those signing it spoke for the people and made it the people's compact by their proxy. But the people make the compact, and their understanding is decisive—otherwise they are not bound by it. We must either assume from the evidence that Jefferson and the people placed the same meaning on the phrase, and everything else in the Declaration, or that Jefferson and the others were defective as representatives for some reason, either intentionally or unintentionally, and the compact written was not the one approved by the people for whom they spoke—and thus is null and void and not part of Americans' political heritage.

Unlike political philosophers' treatises, which can contain hidden or esoteric meanings, public documents that are the basis for common commitments must, under close textual analysis, be read for surface meaning. If the meaning is not apparent to the average reader, then the document does not perform the function for which it was written. Those writing political tracts must be well aware of their audience. Novelty is acceptable only if its basis is already understood and approved. The rhetoric and symbols in the document must be familiar

2. Paul Leicester Ford (ed.), *The Writings of Thomas Jefferson* (10 vols.; New York, 1892–99), X, 343–44.

and widely shared. Therefore we would not likely accept interpretations of the Declaration that would differ from how it was generally read at first.

Even if we are forced to accept the obvious, surface meaning of the document, the source of the ideas is still a matter for debate. For many years the standard interpretation was Carl Becker's, and he saw the Declaration as a direct expression of Locke's ideas. More recently, Garry Wills has argued for the centrality of ideas from the Scottish Enlightenment.[3] Daniel J. Elazar and John Kincaid have proposed that the Declaration fundamentally expresses covenant ideas.[4]

Most of the Declaration of Independence derives directly from the early state constitutions—early state compacts, to be more precise—and thus from the covenant/compact tradition, English common law, and Whig political theory. Much of the language sounds like Locke's because the Americans enthusiastically fastened upon his clear, efficient vocabulary for expressing what they had already been doing for years. In a sense, then, the Declaration is Lockean, but to say nothing more is to miss the document's pedigree and much that is in it. Furthermore, the credit given Locke may with equal or greater force be given Algernon Sidney, who in turn cites most prominently Aristotle, Plato, Roman republican writers, and the Old Testament.

The Declaration as a Social Compact

An examination of the text will confirm this broader pedigree. The textual analysis here does not center on Locke and the Scottish Enlightenment. Those interested should consult Becker and Wills. The point here is to illustrate the links with the state compacts, colonial American political thought derived from covenant theory, Algernon Sidney, and others to establish the manner and extent to which the Declaration of Independence should be viewed as part of a national compact.

The widely read opening paragraphs are less than a fourth of the text. The rest consists mainly of twenty-eight charges against the king justifying the break with Britain. All but four are from state constitutions. On January 5, 1776, six months before the Declaration was written, New Hampshire adopted the first constitution of an independent state. The framers included as a long pre-

3. Carl Becker, *The Declaration of Independence: A Study in the History of Ideas* (New York, 1922); Garry Wills, *Inventing America: Jefferson's Declaration of Independence* (New York, 1978).

4. This position is only beginning to show up in the literature. For the initial statement, see Daniel J. Elazar and John Kincaid, *The Declaration of Independence: The Founding Covenant of the American People,* Temple University's Center for the Study of Federalism monograph (Philadelphia, December, 1980).

amble the reasons why they were declaring their independence. The list contains five of the twenty-eight charges in the Declaration. On March 26, 1776, South Carolina adopted the second new constitution, and since there still was no general declaration of independence, the preamble gave reasons for breaking with Britain. South Carolina's list contained nineteen of the Declaration's twenty-eight charges. On June 29, 1776, Virginia adopted the third state document, and the preamble listed reasons for writing an independent constitution. This list also contains nineteen charges against the king, but in a different combination. South Carolina, Virginia, and New Hampshire, among them, gave twenty-four of the twenty-eight charges.

During the spring of 1776, lists of grievances against the king were regular features in the newspapers. Sometimes the list was a reprinting of one of the early state constitutions, sometimes there were other combinations of grievances. Jefferson did not have to go far to find most of what is in the Declaration.

Consider the following quotation from the Mecklenburg Resolves (North Carolina), published May 31, 1775:

> Resolved: That we do hereby declare ourselves a free and independent people; are and of right ought to be a sovereign and self-governing association, under the control of no power, other than that of our God and the General Government of the Congress: To the maintenance of which Independence we solemnly pledge to each other our mutual cooperation, our Lives, our Fortunes, and our most Sacred Honor.[5]

The last sentence of the Declaration says, "And for the support of this Declaration, with a firm reliance on the Protection of Divine Providence, we mutually pledge to each other our Lives, our Fortunes and our sacred Honor." Together with the background of "all men are created equal," the Declaration of Independence begins to look like an efficiently worded, analytically coherent compendium of ideas from the political literature of the era, just as Jefferson said in his letter to Henry Lee.

In earlier chapters we learned that the covenant-derived compact form of foundation document evolved by English colonists in America usually began by creating a people, explained why the document was necessary, provided a definition of the kind of people they were or hoped to become, created a government, and described that form of government. All but the last two foundation elements are in the Declaration. Furthermore, these compacts tended to put the first foundation elements in a preamble and a bill of rights. As we shall see, the Declaration does so, though with a unique twist.

5. Thorpe (ed.), *Federal and State Constitutions,* V, 2786–87.

The first paragraph tells why the document is needed—the colonies are breaking with Britain and an explanation for such drastic action is due mankind. The first paragraph also refers to the creation of a new people who are dissolving the political bands connecting them with another people. In early colonial covenants and compacts, those who signed were in effect defining the people. The last paragraph of the Declaration says that the signatures are those of the representatives of the "united States of America" acting "in the Name, and by authority of the good People of these Colonies."

The document begs the important question of whether this agreement is among the states, and thus among thirteen separate peoples, or whether it creates one united people at the national level. Evidence in the Declaration supports both sides. For a single people, there are, for example, the opening statement about "one people" separating from another, the capitalized and singular form in the last-paragraph reference to the "good People of these Colonies," and the fact that the signatures are in no particular order and there is no indication of the states from which the men came. At the same time, the plural in the last-paragraph mention of the creation of "Free and Independent States" and the plural reference to the states in the list of grievances, among other items, point to the Declaration as a compact among the states.

The Declaration in a sense contains implicitly the first statement of Americans' dual citizenship. It is interesting, and perhaps significant, that references to the creation of a single people predominate toward the beginning, and that later language is for multiple peoples. The list of grievances refers at times to the king's actions vis-à-vis some of the states, and at other times to things he has done to hurt all Americans.

The source of the ambiguity may lie in the Declaration's simultaneously creating independent states and a combination of these states. The textual ambiguity thus reflects a fundamental aspect of American constitutional politics—the presence of two levels of government, or federalism. If the document had spoken of only one national people, it would have denied the existence of state government, and thus not been acceptable. If it had created only thirteen separate peoples, the document would have made no sense, for the states were making common cause. It is perhaps most useful to view the Declaration as effectively, yet unself-consciously, creating with the same act a national people and thirteen state peoples. The relationship would have to be worked out in the description of institutions for collective decision making, first in the Articles of Confederation and then in the Constitution.

The simultaneous creation of national and state peoples is clear in the title of the document, "The unanimous Declaration of the thirteen united States of America." There are thirteen states, but they are united. Furthermore, the Declaration reflects a unanimity. There is an important point concerning the word *unanimous*. The Declaration that was passed on July 4 was not unanimous, and the word did not appear in the title of the first printed version in July. That version did not have the names affixed at the end so as to protect the signers from British retaliation for as long as possible. New York did not approve it, and not all the eventual signers were present on July 4. On July 15, 1776, New York approved the Declaration, and there was an official signing on August 2. Only fifty men signed then; five more added their names separately during the fall. Finally, on January 18, 1777, the Continental Congress authorized the printing of the Declaration, this time with the signers' names, though the fifty-sixth signature, that of Thomas McKean, had not yet been affixed. The word *unanimous* was added to the title, and this became the official version. It is on display in the National Archives Building.

The change in the title could have been an attempt to put up a united front against Britain. Or the insistence upon unanimity might have been a recognition that a compact does not bind those who do not agree to it. If there is to be a national people, a national social compact, both John Locke and the American constitutional tradition require that the agreement be unanimous. Anyone not signing or agreeing to the compact would not be part of the people it created, leaving those inhabitants of the nonsigning state a separate people. The insistence upon unanimity is evidence that the Declaration of Independence was a social compact. Who were the signers—representatives of the American people or representatives of the people of thirteen independent states? Perhaps the ambiguity of the document on this point was supposed to imply both.

The first paragraph states that upon dissolving the political bands with Britain, the American people take up a "separate and equal station to which the Laws of Nature and Nature's God entitle them." American political literature was full of statements that the American people considered themselves and the British people equal. Every man has the God-given right to grant and to withhold consent. "Nature's God" activates the religious grounding; "Laws of Nature" activates a natural rights theory such as Locke's. The Declaration thus simultaneously appeals to reason and to revelation as the basis for the American right to separate from Britain, create a new and independent people, and be considered equal to any other nation on Earth.

Jefferson was honest when he said that the Declaration did not aim at originality of principles or sentiments. His problem was not philosophical but rhetorical, finding the words in which to cast the argument so that it would gain wide and enthusiastic acceptance. His task was considerably eased since, as Gordon Wood puts it, "[e]nlightened rationalism and evangelical Calvinism were not at odds in 1776; both when interpreted by Whigs placed revolutionary emphasis on the general will of the community and on the responsibility of the collective people to define it." [6] When it came to building and running civil societies, few American Whigs in the 1770s saw any conflict between what they read in Locke or Montesquieu and what they read in the Bible.

When, in paragraph two, the Declaration says, "We hold these truths to be self-evident," the truths were axiomatic on both biblical and rationalist grounds. What are they?

> [A]ll men are created equal, that they are endowed by their Creator with certain unalienable Rights, that among these are Life, Liberty and the Pursuit of Happiness.—That to secure these rights, Governments are instituted among Men, deriving their just powers from the consent of the governed.—That whenever any Form of Government becomes destructive of these ends, it is the Right of the People to alter or abolish it, and to institute new Government, laying its foundation on such principles and organizing its powers in such form, as to them shall seem most likely to effect their Safety and Happiness.

The phrasing appears to be pure Locke, but the words are just as close to those used by a contemporary of Locke's who was usually mentioned in the same breath with him—Algernon Sidney. In his *Discourses Concerning Government* published the year before Locke's *Second Treatise,* Sidney quotes liberally from Aristotle, Plato, the Bible, and the Jesuits Bellarmine and Suárez. [7] The last two, as has been demonstrated by Quentin Skinner in his *Foundations of Modern Political Thought,* were responsible for bringing contract theory to a high point of completion. In fact, most of what Locke has to say is found in their writings. [8] Jefferson could not admit that the Declaration might be in part beholden to the work of two Spanish Jesuits, even if he had read them, which is doubtful. But he did cite Aristotle, Cicero, and Sidney as three thinkers who influenced him, and Sidney frequently quotes Aristotle and the Roman republican thinkers. It is difficult not to conclude that Algernon Sidney was Jefferson's source for seeing these two classical writers as relevant to the Declaration.

The intent here is not to replace Locke with Sidney, or to say that Locke was not important for the Declaration's phraseology. Rather, it is to expand our sense

6. Gordon S. Wood, *The Creation of the American Republic, 1776–1787* (Chapel Hill, 1969), 60.

7. Algernon Sidney, *Discourses Concerning Government* (1698; rpr. New York, 1979). References to Plato, Aristotle, and the Roman writers are found throughout the book, but most concentrated in Chapter II, which is the second 25 percent of the text. Bellarmine and Suárez are most often cited here as well. References to the Bible occur throughout.

8. Quentin Skinner, *The Foundations of Modern Political Thought* (2 vols.; Cambridge, England, 1978), II, 148–66, 318–58.

of the document's background. Sidney is especially interesting, since he combines reason and revelation in his analysis, and thus shows how easily the Declaration can be an expression of earlier, biblically based American constitutional thought.[9]

> That Man is naturally free; That he cannot justly be deprived of that Liberty without cause, and that he doth not resign it, or any part of it, unless it be in consideration of a greater good. (p. 5)

> Is there any absurdity in saying that . . . God in Goodness and Mercy to Mankind, hath with an equal hand given to all the benefit of Liberty, with some measure of understanding of how to use it. (p. 14)

> That 'tis evident in Scripture God hath ordained Powers; but God hath given them to no particular Person, because by Nature all Men are equal; therefore he has given Power to the People or Multitude. (p. 16; quoting Bellarmine)

> Man cannot continue in the perpetual and entire fruition of the Liberty that God hath given him. The Liberty of one is thwarted by that of another; and whilst they are all equal, none will yield to any, otherwise than by a general consent. This is the ground of all just governments. (p. 23)

> If it be said that every Nation ought in this to follow their own Constitutions . . . [t]hey cannot be rightly made, if they are contrary to the universal Law of God and Nature . . . but every people is by God and Nature left to the liberty of regulating these matters relating to themselves according to their own prudence or convenience. (p. 48)

> Civil Society is composed of Equals, and fortified by mutual compact. (p. 68)

> But as Reason is our Nature, that can never be natural to us that is not rational. (p. 72)

> [T]hey who place the Power in a Multitude, understand a Multitude composed of Freemen, who think it for their convenience to join together, and to establish such Laws and Rules as they oblige themselves to observe; which Multitude, whether it be great or small, has the same Right, because ten men are as free as ten millions of men. (p. 75)

That all men are created equal is a position central to Locke's writing, but for a repetitious insistence upon the point, it is to Sidney we should turn. However, the sentiments, ideas, and commitments found in Locke and Sidney existed

9. All quotations are from the original 1698 text.

also in American colonial writing long before these two English theorists published their great works. In particular, credit for first introducing the theory of compacts to the English-speaking world should go to Thomas Hooker, who was largely responsible for the Fundamental Orders of Connecticut. Hooker emphasized popular sovereignty, majority rule, liberty, and separating suffrage from religion. Roger Williams elaborated upon those notions and reduced the theory to a working system in Rhode Island.[10] What has often been called the fruit of the American Revolution was in reality the result of radically extending the logic inherent in the Protestant Reformation, especially as the process occurred in colonial America.[11]

On the other hand, the manner of expressing these ideas and commitments in the Declaration of Independence rested heavily upon the writings of Sidney and Locke, as well as Burlamaqui and Vattel, though mediated by two slightly earlier documents written by prominent Americans.

The phraseology of the Declaration greatly resembles the preamble to the Virginia Constitution, adopted in June, 1776, especially in the list of abuses by the king. The other document upon which Jefferson drew was probably George Mason's Declaration of Rights, which was first published on June 6, 1776, and widely reproduced. Mason, a fellow Virginian, wrote in his first paragraph that "all men are born equally free and independent and have certain inherent natural Rights, of which they can not, by any Compact, deprive or divest their Posterity; among which are the Enjoyment of Life and Liberty, with the Means of Acquiring and possessing property, and pursuing and obtaining Happiness and Safety." Mason then said that sovereignty resides in the people, government exists for the common good and security; and when any government is found unworthy of the trust placed in it, a majority of the community "hath an indubitable, inalienable, and indefensible Right to Reform, alter, or abolish it."[12] As with the phrase "all men are created equal," the broad concepts were long a part of American use, and the phraseology so much in the air breathed by Americans during the 1770s, that Jefferson could not avoid using them.

Even altering Locke's formula "life, liberty, and property" to "life, liberty, and

10. Hooker had an extremely democratic view, and was also influential in the writing of the New England Confederation. In Rhode Island, Williams helped write the Providence Charter (1644), the Acts and Orders of 1647, which united Rhode Island, and the Rhode Island Charter of 1663. His great political tract *The Bloudy Tenent* argued for religious freedom and freedom of conscience in a manner similar to John Milton's *Areopagitica,* which also appeared in 1644.

11. This argument has been notably made by Anson Phelps Stokes in *Church and State in the United States* (New York, 1950), esp. Chap. III.

12. See Julian P. Boyd, *The Declaration of Independence: The Evolution of the Text* (Princeton, 1945), 15.

happiness" was neither a partial rejection nor a basic copying of Locke. George Mason had the formulation, though in a longer phrase, and it was old and widespread. The idea that happiness is the end of government could be found in the writing of John Adams, James Wilson, Alexander Hamilton, George Mason, James Otis, and Richard Bland, to name a few. John Adams said, for example: "Upon this point all speculative politicians will agree, that the happiness of society is the end of government. . . . From this principle it will follow that the form of government which communicates ease, comfort, security, or, in one word, happiness, to the greatest number of persons, and in the greatest degree, is the best."[13] The idea was also in the writings of those from whom these Americans drew, including Burlamaqui, Wollaston, Beccaria, and Bolingbroke.

If there was nothing new in the phrasing and ideas of the Declaration, wherein lies its great significance? First of all, Jefferson summarized the essentials of American political thought with a brevity and an eloquence that take away one's breath. In rhetorical power it has few peers—not only did it help galvanize American resistance to Britain, it continues to excite emotions in America and elsewhere.

Second, the Declaration of Independence was the instrument for breaking from Britain, and it created a new model as well as a universally valid justification for building political societies. Third, it is the document that served to create and define Americans as a people. The Declaration contained the first part of their national compact, defined their basic values and commitments, and was thus essential to the founding of the United States. Fourth, since the Constitution replaced the Articles of Confederation but not the Declaration, Americans still live under a national compact of which the Declaration is a part. The Declaration contains the grounding for the Constitution, as well as the values underlying the American system of government.

The grievances against the king require some examination. Viewed one way, the charges expressed reasons for breaking with Britain. Viewed another way, they listed American political commitments. The first six charges dealt with the legislature and legislative process, which was appropriate given the long-standing American preference for legislative supremacy. The legislature was supposed to engage in a deliberative process to seek the common good. The king had disrupted the legislatures, interfered with their internal workings, dissolved them, called them together under circumstances not conducive to deliberation, placed conditions upon the laws they passed, refused to assent to laws, and failed to enforce ones properly passed. Every one of these charges had the king either explicitly or implicitly threatening, thwarting, or neglecting the common

13. The quotation from Adams, as well as the argument in these paragraphs, is to be found in Ray Forrest Harvey, *Jean Jacques Burlamaqui* (Chapel Hill, 1937), 118.

good of the American people. The third charge was notable also for expressing a strong desire for continued westward expansion, and the sixth charge for upholding the people's right to assemble peaceably and to petition their representatives.

According to the seventh charge, the king had interfered with immigration to America. Freedom of movement, commitment to an easy naturalization process, a view of immigration as positive rather than negative, and a commitment to westward expansion were all part of this paragraph.

Charges eight and nine had to do with the king's interference in the judicial process. The Americans here asserted their preference for separating the judiciary from executive control.

The tenth charge stated the American attachment to frugality as an essential principle of government. They objected to the swarms of officers not out of opposition to a bureaucracy, but because these men would "eat out their substance," that is, use up too much of the common wealth.

English common law contained a prohibition against a standing army in times of peace. Also, the military was to be subordinate to the civil power. A soldier was therefore subject to both military tribunals and civil courts of law, and if there was a conflict, the civil court was to prevail. Further, troops were not to be quartered among the people in peacetime. The eleventh, twelfth, fourteenth, and fifteenth charges held that the king had contravened these tenets of common law. The Americans enunciated their preference for a citizen militia and for civil control of the military, prefiguring the Second Amendment.

Halfway through the list, it should be apparent that this amounts to a bill of rights. It set forth a self-definition of the people created by the document, and it enunciated basic values and commitments. One thread running through the entire list was a commitment to two levels of government. Most of the charges dealt with the king's actions against one or several of the states rather than against all of them. The strong implication is a commitment to protect state government, prefiguring the republican guarantee clause of the U.S. Constitution.

The thirteenth charge is in certain respects what the Declaration is all about. The king had joined with Parliament to make laws for the colonies when the colonies had their own legislatures. If a colonial legislature levied a tax, that was fine since it was the colonists' own creation, their own government, doing so. But if Parliament levied a tax affecting Americans, this was taxation without representation and a crime against all of America. Reflected here is a fundamental political commitment: Government is based upon the consent of the governed and is beholden to the majority, or liberty has been extinguished.

The sixteenth and seventeenth charges were precise glosses upon the thirteenth. American trade with the rest of the world was subject to a host of parliamentary regulations that dated back to the Navigation Act of 1660. These charges are a further statement of government by consent, but they are also antimercantilist and uphold the principle of free trade.

English common law included many guarantees that had to do with trial by jury. Charges eighteen and nineteen argued that Americans had been denied that right in a variety of ways. The commitment to jury trials was here expressed, and became part of the Constitution. The next charge referred to the Roman legal system instituted in Quebec in place of the common law, and the geographical extension of Quebec into what later became the Northwest Territories of the United States. This last was a threat to westward expansion, the commitment to which was in the seventh charge.

The twenty-first and twenty-second charges expressed once again the fundamental commitment to government by the people's consent. If charters of government can be ignored, important laws altered, the form of government changed, and legislatures suspended, what has become of popular sovereignty, popular consent, and majority rule? After one hundred fifty years of constitutional theory as practiced in America, the rejection of such behavior affirmed some of the most fundamental of all American commitments.

The next five charges listed all the ways that the king had made war on the colonists. Together these expressed one of government's most important jobs—to protect the people from foreign and domestic violence. In effect, the king had withdrawn his protection and thereby failed to provide the most basic service for which government is created. The implication was that the king had broken the ties, not the colonists.

The twenty-eighth charge, and the long paragraph that follows, revealed the American commitment to deliberative processes. Echoing an earlier paragraph, in which it is stated that men should not lightly undertake important changes in government and that they should pursue all avenues before having to make drastic changes, the Declaration here notes that the colonists have tried all means, legal and informal, for solving the problems. All their attempts had been rebuffed or ignored. So many abuses, just enumerated, had finally eroded Americans' patience and exhausted the deliberative process.

The last paragraph contained another interesting phrase. Any document calling on God as a witness would technically be a covenant. As has been argued, American constitutionalism had its roots in the covenant form that was secularized into the compact. The last paragraph of the Declaration says: "[A]ppealing to the Supreme Judge of the world for the rectitude of our intentions, do, in the Name, and by authority of the good People of these Colonies." One could argue that with God as a witness, the Declaration of Independence is in fact a covenant. The wording is peculiar, however, and the form of an oath is present, but the words stop short of what is normally expected. But the juxtaposition of a near oath and the words about popular sovereignty is an intricate dance around the covenant/compact form. The Declaration of Independence may be a covenant; it is definitely part of a compact.

10. The Articles of Confederation

The Anti-Federalists have been consigned to the ranks of those who merely opposed. Academics have largely dismissed them as "men of little faith," and the rest of America has forgotten them. Emphasis upon a comprehensive recovery of the American founding has only slightly improved Americans' view of the Anti-Federalists. Symptomatic of the situation, perhaps, is the publication by Herbert J. Storing of *The Complete Anti-Federalist*. The first of the seven volumes is entitled *What the Anti-Federalists Were For*, as if anything positive in their stance requires some explaining. Perhaps unnoticed, and certainly unremarked in the reviews, Storing's collection further undermines the image of the Anti-Federalists by gathering in one place anything negative they had to say.[1]

Yet these Anti-Federalists had a coherent, positive view of politics that stressed liberty, popular sovereignty, majority rule, deliberative processes, localism, and a whole host of ideas and commitments central to American political theory. Further, they wrote more than two dozen state constitutions; successfully prosecuted a war of liberation against a world power; generated thousands of political pamphlets, tracts, and newspaper essays; and provided most of what eventually would go into the United States Constitution. If we were to collect all the writings from the 1770s and 1780s by those later placed in the category "Anti-Federalist," the essays against the Constitution would be but a marginal percentage of the total. Yet this small portion is how the Anti-Federalists are remembered.

Imagine, for example, that the Federalists were those opposed to the Articles of Confederation, and thus might be termed "Anticonfederationists." Then collections would include everything they had to say against the Articles and ignore all other writings by Hamilton, Madison, Jay, and others. Whatever was

1. Herbert J. Storing (ed.), *The Complete Anti-Federalist* (7 vols.; Chicago, 1981).

excluded would not be reprinted. The net result would be that the Federalists were remembered as crabby, negative, unimaginative men of little faith.

Nor has there been anything resembling a "boomlet" of publications on the Articles of Confederation. We still rely on the excellent yet solitary work of Merrill Jensen published decades ago. Properly perceived as an inadequate constitution for post-1780s America, the Articles has also been written off as unimportant and uninteresting. The document does have a place as the Americans' first national constitution, as part of their first national compact, and as the instrument upon which the present United States Constitution was directly built.

Early Plans for Union

Despite English colonists' distinct lack of interest in uniting their colonies under one government, there were many such plans. The New England Confederation (1643), written by the colonists, was the first. It was typical of plans the colonists wrote, since there was a need for common security and the confederation essentially preserved the independence of local governments. The Commission of the Council for Foreign Plantations (1660) was typical of plans of union devised in Britain. It was predicated upon mercantilist principles of economic development for the colonies and enhanced revenue for Britain, and at the same time it was somewhat indifferent to the colonists' political institutions.

Later plans included the Royal Commission to Governor Andros to unite all of New England, New York, and the Jerseys (1688); William Penn's Plan of Union (1696); the report of the Board of Trade on union of New York with other colonies (1696); the D'Avenant Plan (1698); a Virginian's plan, in "An Essay on the Government of the English Plantations on the Continent of America" (1701); the Livingston Plan (1701); the Earl of Stair's Proposals (1721); Plan of the Lords of Trade (1721); Daniel Cox's Plan, in "A Description of the English province of Carolina" (1722); the Kennedy Plan (1751); the Franklin Plan of 1751; Richard Peter's Plan (1754); Hutchinson's Plan (1754); the Albany Plan of Union (1754); Plan of the Lords of Trade (1754); Dr. Samuel Johnson's Plan (1760); the Galloway Plan (1774); and Franklin's Articles of Confederation (1775).

In Massachusetts, Connecticut, and Rhode Island, specific documents produced federations, such as the Fundamental Orders of Connecticut (1639) and the Acts and Orders of 1647 in Rhode Island. Attempts at regionwide confederations seem a natural extension, as does a confederation uniting all the colonies. However, the American Whigs' devotion to local control made them highly resistant to confederations larger than a single state. These ideas and plans for a united America were not without consequence. Each addressed the issues, some with success, that would continue to exercise national politics through the 1787 Constitutional Convention—indeed, until the 1860s.

To illustrate the connection between postrevolutionary America and colonial developments, let us examine briefly the Albany Plan of Union. In June, 1754, the Board of Trade in London called for a congress of American colonies to discuss mutual defense. Britain was clearly on the verge of a major war with France, and the war was expected to spill over into North America (later called the French and Indian Wars). It was felt that without a collective effort the colonists would be no match for the French, especially since the French would likely mobilize their Indian allies. In addition, the delegates were to negotiate with the Iroquois Confederacy and thus undercut the French advantage.

Seven colonies sent delegates to Albany—New Hampshire, Massachusetts, Rhode Island, Connecticut, New York, Pennsylvania, and Maryland. Negotiations with the Iroquois were not successful, as the Indians later sided with the French, but a little-appreciated effect of the meeting was to bring the colonists in direct contact with a successful confederation.[2] The lesson was not lost: at least three confederation plans were presented at the Albany congress. One was written by Benjamin Franklin. After considerable discussion, the delegates adopted the plan as their major recommendation for mutual defense and termed it the Albany Plan of Union.[3] The congress not only set a precedent for later continental colonial meetings, it also provided the first version of a united colonial government resulting from a trans-colonial political process. The procedure was similar during the Stamp Act crisis and then the Continental Congresses in the 1770s.

Unlike the Iroquois model, Franklin's plan did not provide each colony a veto. Instead, the plan was a logical extension of the American colonial pattern of political organization. There was an executive, the president general, appointed by the Crown. The legislature, called the Grand Council, controlled the purse strings, though the president general also had to sign all legislation. The typical colonial pattern—a royal governor locked in combat with a legislature elected by the colonists—was thus reproduced on the "national" level. Since by this time the legislatures had gained the upper hand in the colonies, the same was expected to occur eventually on the trans-colonial level.

The united legislature was empowered to write and regulate treaties with the Indians (making peace and declaring war); regulate trade with the Indians; provide for troops, forts, ships, and anything else to defend any colony (though

2. See Bruce E. Johansen, *Forgotten Founders: Benjamin Franklin, the Iroquois and the Rationale for the American Revolution* (Ipswich, Mass., 1982).

3. The text is in Albert H. Smyth (ed.), *The Writings of Benjamin Franklin* (10 vols.; New York, 1907), III, 8–29.

the consent of a colony's legislature was required to raise troops within it); create and regulate new settlements until their own government was granted by charter from the king; and, most important, raise money through duties and taxes "collected with the least inconvenience to the people; rather discouraging luxury than loading industry with unnecessary burdens." [4] The proposed government would have had the same general powers that were granted under the Articles of Confederation.

The Albany Plan was superior to the Articles in the design of the legislature. Elected every three years, the representatives would be apportioned according to each colony's financial contributions. Thus the colonies would be arguing for a decrease in representation every time they asked for a lower tax levy. Linking taxes to commerce and wealth effectively meant overrepresentation for smaller colonies, since they had disproportionately fewer citizens in low-income-producing frontier situations. The southern colonies were also overrepresented. The plan took into account the commercial effects of slavery, but did not deal with the question that would arise if population was the base—should slaves be included in the head count?

The apportionment proposed for the first three years until tax contributions could be worked out illustrates Franklin's shrewd calculations about probable future politics in a united legislature. The Grand Council was to have the following members:

Probable New England Coalition
    New Hampshire 2
    Massachusetts 7
    Rhode Island 2
    Connecticut 5
Probable Middle State Coalition
    New York 4
    West and East New Jersey 3
    Pennsylvania 6
    Maryland 4
Probable Southern State Coalition
    Virginia 7
    North Carolina 4
    South Carolina 4
              Total 48

Four of the eleven colonies could create a majority, but that was unlikely because the three largest colonies were each the centerpiece of a different political

4. *Ibid.*, 18.

subculture. The most likely coalitions were not large versus small colonies, but rather a New England coalition centered on Massachusetts, a southern coalition centered on Virginia, and a middle coalition centered on Pennsylvania. Since Franklin was a Pennsylvanian, it is not surprising that Pennsylvania would probably be disproportionately influential. It is also of some interest that the seats apportioned to the southern colonies in effect counted slaves at roughly three-fifths of a person.

The Albany Plan of Union was rejected by the Crown as undercutting its authority, and the colonial legislatures were unwilling to sacrifice any of their power. The weakness of Whig political theory with regard to "national" union thus appeared more than twenty years before the Articles of Confederation. Americans consistently preferred local control to distant political entities. The same perspective that later necessitated the break with a tyrannical Britain also fueled a suspicion that any continental government was a source of danger as well, even if that government used standard Whig institutions.

It is an irony of history that in the Articles of Confederation the American Whigs opted for something closer to the Iroquois Confederacy than to their own state systems as represented by Franklin's plan. Further, during the debate in the Continental Congress, Franklin's plan was proposed as an alternative. Had it been adopted, the need for replacement would likely have arisen long after 1787. In the long run, the form of government proposed by Franklin would probably have evolved into a parliamentary system similar to Britain's.

The Place of the Articles of Confederation

On October 7, 1777, the Continental Congress voted on whether the states under the Articles of Confederation should have one vote for every fifty thousand inhabitants. Only Pennsylvania and Virginia voted in favor. The next proposal was one vote for every thirty thousand inhabitants. Only Virginia voted for it, though the two North Carolina delegates split their vote and John Adams cast one of Massachusetts' three votes in favor. On the proposal that representation be proportional to a state's taxes paid to the national treasury, Virginia voted in favor, one of the three South Carolina delegates voted in favor, and John Adams once again cast his minority vote in support. Finally, on the proposal to give each state one vote, only the Virginia delegation voted no. North Carolina split, and negative votes were cast by one South Carolina delegate and by John Adams.[5]

It is easy to write off the Virginia vote as the desire of a large state to double its proportional representation, but this fails to account for the other large states' consistent support of "one state, one vote." During the debate, John Witherspoon of New Jersey clearly set forth the view of compacts that was the basis of

5. These votes are recorded in W. C. Ford *et al.* (eds.), *Journals of the Continental Congress, 1774–1789* (34 vols.; Washington, D.C., 1904–1937), IX, 779–82.

the opposition.[6] He saw each state as equivalent to an individual, and thus the national government was a compact between individual states, each a self-sufficient community. The Continental Congress would only ever deal with the state as a whole, so that should be the unit of representation. In addition, there was no basis for one state having a greater vote than another. Implicit in Witherspoon's position was the notion of a moral equivalence between communities, regardless of size. He was a minister reared and educated in Scotland. The biblical covenant idea was at the core of his world view. At another point, in the debate on how to levy taxes, Witherspoon said, "[W]e are now entering into a new compact and therefore stand on original ground."[7] Locke would have approved, but Witherspoon's point of reference was the Bible.

Essential to Witherspoon's position was not that states should each have one vote, but that the national government should act upon the states. Since individuals are part of a community, it makes little sense for government to act upon anything other than the community. To act upon individuals is to imply the partial destruction of the community. The stance of American Whigs emphasized community, especially local communities. When it came to designing government at the national level, Whigs thought preserving local communities more important than having a legislature that reflected the community in detail and was supreme. Witherspoon clearly distinguished between what he called a "federal union," in which the members would remain largely independent, and what he called an "incorporating union," which would create a new community of all the individuals in the nation. Given a choice, he preferred the former.

John Adams saw the need for a different model. The question was not "what we are now but what we ought to be when our bargain shall be made." He saw the confederation as creating a new community, a new individual. He spoke of melting pieces of metal into a common mass such that "we shall no longer retain our separate individuality, but become a single individual as to all questions submitted to the confederacy." The national government would act directly upon each individual rather than upon states. Adams here used the Whig perspective to emphasize a national community in which "the interests within doors should be mathematically representative of the interests without doors."[8] Adams was echoing *The Essex Result*, as had Witherspoon. An inherent contradiction within Whig political theory became clear for the first time, and prominent, sincere Whigs were coming down on different sides of the split.

Adams used words that sound much like Madison's later in *The Federalist*. Adams wanted to represent interests, not communities. Proportional represen-

6. *Ibid.*, VI, 1079, 1082, 1101, 1103.
7. *Ibid.*, 1101.
8. *Ibid.*, 1099–1100, 1104.

tation in legislatures was a surrogate for representing the common wealth and thus the interests of a community, since "it is the number of labourers which produce the surplus for taxation, and numbers therefore indiscriminately are the fair index of wealth." Adams said elsewhere in the debate that "the numbers of people were taken by this article [Article XI of the proposed Articles] as an index of the wealth of the state and not as subjects of taxation." Adams had not yet faced the full implications of his "melted metal" theory, according to which individuals would indeed be subject to direct taxation.[9] The U.S. Constitution later reflected this inconsistency: the national government acts directly upon individual citizens, but there can be no direct "head taxes." It took the Sixteenth Amendment to bring about consistency in this regard.

Adams thus backed Franklin's position that representation and taxation should be proportional. He also agreed that analyzing interests, even with the state as the unit of analysis, does not produce a large-state/small-state split. Both Adams and Franklin saw Virginia, Pennsylvania, and Massachusetts as natural leaders of coalitions based upon regional political subcultures rather than upon size. James Wilson, supporting proportional representation, said that "we are not so many states; we are one large state." He concluded finally that "I defy the wit of man to invent a possible case, or to suggest any one thing on earth, which shall be for the interests of Virginia, Pennsylvania, and Massachusetts, and which will not also be for the interest of the other states." Benjamin Rush used another Whig argument, that of pursuing the common good: "I would not have it understood that I am pleading the cause of Pennsylvania; when I entered that door, I considered myself a citizen of America."[10] Implied was the national government's direct connection to the individual person, as was the idea of Americans having a dual citizenship. Franklin, Adams, Wilson, and other future Federalists of note were working out the shift from traditional Whig theory to a theory more suitable for national union, but they were not yet strong enough to prevail. It remained for *experience* with the operation of the Articles to convert enough minds to push for the critical change—having the national government operate directly upon individuals.

Another feature of the debate over representation under the Articles of Confederation was the justification for bicameralism. Roger Sherman began by supporting the states-as-communities position: "We are representatives of States, not individuals." After a few statements that numbers should not be the basis for representation, he suddenly veered to the idea of bicameralism: "The vote should be taken two ways; call the Colonies, and call the individuals, and have a majority of both." In Jefferson's notes on the debate, Samuel Chase of

9. *Ibid.,* 1100, 1099.
10. *Ibid.,* 1106, 1081.

Maryland proposed a slightly different basis for bicameralism. He was recorded as saying that "the smaller states should be secured in all questions concerning life or liberty, and the greater ones in all respecting property . . . in votes relating to money, the voice of each colony should be proportioned to the number of its inhabitants."[11] *The Essex Result* summarized the contrary position—the upper house protects property while the lower house protects lives and rights. Underscoring the lack of coherence in Chase's position were his votes against every proposal for proportional representation. In any event, no argument for bicameralism was heeded. Most delegates to the Continental Congress were thinking defensively. They were too concerned with preserving state political power to take seriously a reasonable argument to make the national government effective, and therefore powerful.

On June 11, 1776, the Continental Congress created a committee to write up articles of confederation. The debate on the proposal continued intermittently in Congress as the committee made presentations from time to time. The final version was adopted November 15, 1777, and on June 26, 1778, a form for ratification by the states was adopted. Eight states signed almost immediately, but other ratifications went on until March 1, 1781, when Maryland became the last to ratify. The next day, Congress assembled for the first time under the Articles of Confederation, America's first national constitution.

The text of the document looked both forward and backward.[12] The first line said "we the undersigned" in the traditional style. At the end, there was a list of signatures in the form commonly used during the colonial era. They were grouped by state. At the beginning, there were two lists of the states in geographical order from north to south, underscoring that state delegates made the agreement, not individuals. In Article I, for the first time in American documentary history, is the phrase "The United States of America." It also reinforced the nature of the parties to this agreement—as did Article II, which said that each state would retain its sovereignty and any powers not expressly granted to the United States. This affirmed the existing state governments, prefiguring the Tenth Amendment as well.

The Articles of Confederation so emphasized the compact between the states that the framers felt a need to add reminders that they were indeed engaged in a common cause as well. Articles III and IV referred to the states entering into "a firm league of friendship" to "perpetuate mutual friendship and intercourse." The preamble called the document "articles of Confederation and perpetual Union," and the last was mentioned again in Article XIII.

11. *Ibid.,* 1081, 1102.

12. The text of the Articles of Confederation is as reproduced in Francis N. Thorpe (ed.), *The Federal and State Constitutions, Colonial Charters, and Other Organic Laws of the United States* (7 vols.; Washington, D.C., 1907), I, 9–17.

The Articles had echoes of colonial documents. For example, Article IV said in part, "No State shall be represented in Congress by less than two, nor by more than seven members"—the range suggested by Franklin in the Albany Plan of Union in 1754, and more or less followed in later national congresses. The same article also echoed Franklin's idea for three-year terms insofar as no delegate could serve more than three one-year terms over any six-year period. In practice, the average delegate served for three years and then was off for three years. This and the prohibition against holding several offices at once were common provisions in state constitutions.

Of even greater interest is the extent to which the Articles of Confederation contained what was in the 1787 Constitution. The general impression is that the Articles was wholly replaced in 1787, but in fact from one-half to two-thirds of what was in the Articles showed up in the 1787 document.

For example, Sections 1 and 2 of Article IV in the present United States Constitution come almost entirely from Article IV of the Articles of Confederation, including "full faith and credit," "privileges and immunities," and the return of interstate fugitives. The admission of new states (Article IV, Section 3) had its counterpart in Article X. The republican guarantee (Article IV, Section 4) was in Article III. Article IX of the Articles granted Congress specific power, not as broad but structurally similar to that in the Constitution. Toward the end of Article IX, the list of prohibitions on national powers resembles that found in Article I, Section 9 of the Constitution. Article VI contained prohibitions on state governments that paralleled to a degree Article I, Section 10.

Article IV in the Articles of Confederation said that "the free inhabitants of each of these States . . . shall be entitled to all the privileges and immunities of free citizens in the several States." These were enumerated: the abilities to move between states, to engage in trade and commerce on an equal footing with the other citizens in the state to which one moved, to be subject to the same taxes and restrictions as other citizens of the state, and to move one's property out of a state (and thus into another state). The implication was that these privileges and immunities existed because there was a United States of America, a national government. Their extent constituted the basis for a national citizenship (one carried these abilities across state lines) and implied a state citizenship as well.

The Articles set up what amounts to a national court system (Article IX), but the system functioned only to adjudicate disputes between states, not individuals. Congress could pass no laws directly affecting individuals, and thus the national court had no jurisdiction over individuals. But when Congress was given such power in the 1787 Constitution, the notion of dual citizenship was revolutionized.

The invention of dual citizenship in the Articles of Confederation, and then the transfer of this concept to the national Constitution in Article VI, Section 2, was the legal basis for the operation of federalism in all its many manifestations. The Articles of Confederation was like a vessel waiting to be filled. Its contents suggested what was needed to provide for a strong and effective national government. And when the new substance of the United States Constitution was added, the older vessel to a significant degree determined its final shape.

Aside from the narrower grant of power to Congress, and a unicameral legislature in which each state had one vote, the Articles differed from the United States Constitution mainly in placing the Court directly under Congress and in having the Committee of the States (one delegate from each state) instead of a single executive. Characteristic of state constitutions were a weak executive, often under the sway of a committee appointed or elected by the legislature, and a court system directly under the legislature. The Articles of Confederation in these respects was not the result of independent theorizing about the best institutions. It was a straightforward extension of Whig political thought to national government.

The looseness of the confederation and its inherent weakness were reasonably close to the Iroquois Confederacy except in one important respect. The Iroquois Confederacy required unanimity for concerted action; the Articles of Confederation required unanimity only for amending the document. Otherwise, nine states had to approve normal legislation and the admission of new states, and nine of the states on the Committee of the States had to approve exercise of any of its powers.

Why did the Founders require nine states to ratify the Constitution rather than thirteen or a majority of seven? Experience, and the likelihood that Rhode Island would not ratify, made unanimity an impractical alternative. A simple majority of seven might not have included the large states, and the new nation would have been crippled from the start. There was, however, considerable experience with a nine-state requirement in the Continental Congress. As inefficacious as the Articles of Confederation had been, it had structured the standard for agreement. Nine states constituted a two-thirds majority. Although such a majority was at times extremely difficult to construct, a provision that satisfied nine invariably satisfied more than nine. This was a litmus test the Framers understood, and the two-thirds majority required by the Articles led them to adopt a similar requirement for ratifying the Constitution. If it worked, they would have an extended republic. If they could not get nine to approve, they were better off sticking with the defective national government they already had.

Without the Articles of Confederation, the extended republic would have had to be invented out of the writings of Europeans as a rank experiment that a skeptical public would likely not accept. And the rule for ratification would have been based on something other than reasonable expectations derived from experience. On the other hand, Americans had learned that government on a continental basis was possible, in certain respects desirable, and that a stable, effective national government required more than an extended republic—it needed power that could be applied directly to individuals. Experience also convinced them that the national government should have limited powers, and that state governments could not be destroyed. There was a logic to experience that no amount of reading in political theory could shake.

Providing for an amendment process was one of the most innovative aspects of both national constitutions. Equally innovative was the provision for admitting new states. History demonstrated that a nation adding new territory almost invariably treated it as conquered land. Even when new units were accepted as equals, they were previously existing states. The Founders proposed the future addition, on an equal footing, of new states from territories now sparsely settled, if settled at all. Today Americans take that possibility for granted, but the Articles of Confederation is of major historical importance for first containing this extraordinarily liberal provision, which became part of the U.S. Constitution. It guaranteed the building of an extended republic.

If the Articles of Confederation already defined an extended republic, what was the major advantage of the Constitution? Why did Madison make so much of something already in a document he did not respect? He did so because the national government would affect the citizens of this extended republic *directly*. It was the combination that produced the effect Madison wanted.

Madison may have borrowed the language of David Hume to describe the advantages of an extended republic, but the fact existed in the Articles of Confederation, and his own experience as a citizen had to be decisive. Furthermore, living under the Articles provided him with the best possible school for understanding the crucial element for a stable, effective government in an extended republic—a direct connection between the national government and its citizens. The state governments would have to be retained, which necessarily implied dual citizenship.

The Declaration of Independence and the Articles of Confederation together formed Americans' first national compact. The Declaration of Independence and the United States Constitution together form the second national compact, under which Americans live today. The first one was based on a coherent political theory, American Whiggism. The second also had a coherent theory behind it, American federalism. The second theory, like the second compact, did not so much replace the first as evolve from it, a revision of an earlier experiment found to be flawed. As we will see, that was still subject to future revision. The United States was not founded in 1787; the nation was refounded upon a base that had been laid earlier.

11.   The Context of the Constitution

One danger in stressing connections and continuities is giving the impression that the process was smooth, inevitable, and predictable. The continuities did not result from simple adherence to tradition or in any sense reflect control by earlier generations. Rather, each generation, when faced with a situation of founding or refounding, used what still made sense to them from the past and added or made up whatever they thought was needed and would work. That is, the continuities resulted from the stable characteristics of the people, their commitments, and their circumstances. To the extent that the people and their circumstances changed, so was there experimentation in American constitutionalism.

Certainly the break with Britain was a major change in circumstances and thus a major impetus to political innovation. At the same time, important aspects of American existence did not change. It will therefore be possible, in an examination of the Constitution, to identify much that is familiar without denying what is new.

First, we must rid ourselves of the widely accepted notion that James Madison was *the* Founder. We rely heavily upon his writing, especially in *The Federalist* and his notes on the Constitutional Convention proceedings; the power and clarity of his mind can only impress. In a sense, deifying Madison does him an injustice, since some of what is most impressive about his work depends on our seeing that he was one of many founders. For example, we have to admire not only his stamina and memory but also his staggering honesty in reporting the discussion at the convention. Only his notes allow us to say with certainty that the position Madison initially defended, the Virginia Plan, lost rather badly, and that most of what he proposed, supported, or voted for also lost.[1] In short,

---

1. Forrest McDonald says that of the seventy-one proposals that Madison introduced or argued for during the convention, forty were defeated. Also, Madison's preferred constitu-

Madison's own notes are the proof that he was not the primary framer of the Constitution, but was part of a process that prominently involved many others.

Our high opinion of this man has to soar when we read his contributions to *The Federalist*. Defending a proposed constitution that is not his and that in many important respects is at variance with his strongly held opinions, Madison accurately describes what is in the document and how it is likely to work. He also provides a coherent, historically important theory to underpin the Constitution. That theory leads us to consider him *the* Founder. We must, however, decide how useful the theory is. In effect, we the modern readers of the texts create Madison as *the* Founder by accepting as definitive his theoretical explanation of the Constitution. He has become the accepted interpreter of that which he did not write.

Elevating James Madison to the status of primary founder because of his writing in *The Federalist* requires that we ignore what he tells us in his notes on the convention. Furthermore, it requires that we ignore Herbert J. Storing's article in which he notes the extent to which the writings of the other Federalists were neither as extreme nor as coherent as Madison's.[2] In *Federalist 10*, Madison summarized neither the main discussion during the convention nor the public writings of the dozens of other prominent Federalists. Rather, he was providing a *post hoc* theoretical explanation that had considerable originality, the importance of which lies in his trenchant analysis of how all the institutions will work as a system, not upon his summarizing the reasoning of the men at the convention or of his own thinking as one of the authors of the document.

Just as there was no dominant person during the convention, there was no dominant faction. Forrest McDonald finds two broad factions, which he likens roughly to "the court party" and "the country party." Cutting across this factional alignment was an important tripartite split according to the delegates' views of the English constitution. McDonald shows that the supposed large-state/small-state split was more a function of which states had major territorial claims rather than of size per se; it tended to crosscut the other two factional alignments. In addition, there *was* on some issues a large-state/small-state division, and on others a north/south split, not to mention regional coalitions.[3]

At least one-third of the slaveowners came from the northern states. Large-scale land speculators tended to split down the middle on matters relevant to

---

tion had only a limited overlap with the document that was finally adopted. See his *Novus Ordo Seclorum: The Intellectual Origins of the Constitution* (Lawrence, Kans., 1985), 205–209.

2. Herbert J. Storing, "The 'Other' Federalist Papers: A Preliminary Sketch," *Political Science Reviewer*, VI (1976), 215–47.

3. McDonald, *Novus Ordo Seclorum*, 186–224.

their interests. Among the many remaining factional alignments, whether based upon ideological commitment or economic interest, the most important was that each delegate tended to vote for the interests of his respective state, though state delegations often were divided. In sum, the convention resembled pluralist America, with all the divisions then emerging.

Also we must recognize the extent to which those who wrote the Constitution relied upon *experience* more than anything else. To the Founders experience meant, first of all, others' systematic observations about political events in the past. They generally read Plutarch, Livy, Tacitus, and other Roman historians as part of the classical education at the time. Events in ancient Greece and Rome, Renaissance Italian city-states, and modern European history were part of what was included under experience. Hume's *History of England,* Tacitus' *Histories,* and the works of Pufendorf, to name just a few of the historians they read, helped extend the Founders' direct experience across cultures and over time. These historians also tended to reinforce the Whig perspective on the value of republican government.

Aside from formal histories, the Founders also counted among their experience institutions that previous generations had tried and tested. Their respect for the English constitution and the common law was based upon the value accorded the collective experience of generations. They similarly respected the institutions they brought with them from the colonial era and early nationhood. As much as Britain served as a model, the absence of a written British constitution forced the Founders to rely more heavily upon American documents. As a result, the United States Constitution has more in common with the Massachusetts Constitution of 1780 than with the British constitution, no matter how one interprets the latter. The early state constitutions and the colonial documents behind them were the repository of the experience of people whose values and commitments were similar to those of the men at the convention. As unhappy as some delegates were with the state constitutions, the documents represented a source of experience that could not be ignored.

Experience included also living under the state constitutions and the Articles of Confederation. Past institutions had a certain validity, but the founding generation had to test that validity anew. How did the institutions work in the present? Most of the delegates to the convention had served in state or continental legislatures. Many had helped write or amend the state constitutions or the Articles of Confederation.

The delegates were deeply experienced in politics. They had a good sense of what would and would not work, what would and would not be acceptable to the general population. Further, they also tended to seek compromise and could develop the necessary positions for doing so effectively. Upon all these levels of experience the Founders drew. There was one more—the convention itself.

An important, yet often misunderstood vote took place the first day of the convention. The delegates voted to follow a rule of secrecy. Some have seen this as an attempt by elites to keep their perfidious doings from the general public, but the intent was otherwise. Many delegates felt that being away from public scrutiny, they could take positions and make arguments and change their minds later in view of what they learned from the discussion. That is in fact what happened. Relatively free of cant and posturing, the discussion ebbed and flowed as positions shifted, issues were raised over and over again, and compromises made. This final level of experience, the testing of their reactions to arguments, ideas, and personalities, rather than to the imperatives of constituencies, press, and public opinion, should not be minimized. The vote for the rule of secrecy was ultimately a vote for reliance upon direct, unfiltered experience.

The Relevance of European Thinkers

Over the century and a half preceding the Declaration of Independence, colonists developed a set of political institutions that were Whig-like in their operation, and they borrowed English Whig theory to justify institutions they already possessed.[4] The colonists viewed both John Locke and Algernon Sidney as English Whigs, and both theorists were pressed into service. In the process of appropriating this theory, the colonists adapted it to their own needs and experiences. Beginning in the 1760s with the Stamp Act crisis, the colonists borrowed more and more from European political theory as they self-consciously sought justification for their causes and prevailing institutions. New strains of thinking began to enter the picture as well.

Chief among these new strains was Enlightenment theory in its various guises. Members of the founding generation had a large dose of the Scottish Enlightenment in their education, but Continental theorists such as Montesquieu also loomed large. Whig political theory peaked in influence during the writing of the state constitutions in the 1770s and early 1780s. Thereafter Enlightenment writers became increasingly influential, along with the great common law writers. The word *influential* is used advisedly, since the tendency remained for Americans to appropriate piecemeal from each author or to transform what was borrowed.

Thus, for example, it is doubtful that Americans needed Montesquieu to convince them of the virtues of separation of powers, or Hume to persuade them to seek an extended republic. Americans would have pursued both on the basis of their colonial and early national experience, even if Montesquieu and Hume had never written. Americans used their works to transform preferences into coherent theory, and thus to undergird familiar institutions. At the same time, these foreign-bred ideas were pressing Americans to think more deeply, recon-

4. Donald S. Lutz, *Popular Consent and Popular Control: Whig Political Theory in the Early State Constitutions* (Baton Rouge, 1980), 218–25.

sider their commitments and institutions, and seek a more secure political grounding for the future.

The relative influence of European thinkers on American political thought is a large and complex question not to be answered in any but a provisional way here. We can, however, identify the broad trends of influence and which European thinkers need to be especially considered. One means to this end is an examination of the citations in public political literature written between 1760 and 1805.[5] If we ask which book was most frequently cited in that literature, the answer is, the Bible. Table 1 shows that the biblical tradition accounted for roughly one-third of the citations in the sample. However, the sample includes about one-third of all significant secular publications, but only about one-tenth of the reprinted sermons. Even with this undercount, Saint Paul is cited about as frequently as Montesquieu and Blackstone, the two most-cited secular authors, and Deuteronomy is cited almost twice as often as all of Locke's writings put together. A strictly proportional sample with respect to secular and religious sources would have resulted in an abundance of religious references.

About three-fourths of all references to the Bible came from reprinted sermons. The other citations to the Bible came from secular works and, if taken alone, would represent 9 percent of all citations—about equal to the percentage for classical writers. Although the citations came from virtually every part of the Bible, Saint Paul was the favorite in the New Testament, especially the parts of his Epistle to the Romans in which he discusses the basis for and limits on obedience to political authorities. Saint Peter was next, and then John's Gospel. Deuteronomy was the most-cited Old Testament book, followed by Isaiah, Genesis, Exodus, and Leviticus. As one might expect, the authors referred most frequently to the sections about covenants and God's promises to Israel, as well as to similar passages in Joshua, I and II Samuel, I and II Kings, and Matthew's Gospel.[6]

The prominence of ministers in the political literature of the period attests to the continuing influence of religion during the founding era. Table 1 shows, however, a peak period of biblical citation in the 1770s. The movement toward independence found the clergy out in front, and they were also most vigorous in maintaining morale during the war. Approximately 80 percent of the political

5. See Donald S. Lutz, "The Relative Influence of European Writers on Late Eighteenth-Century American Political Thought," *American Political Science Review,* LXXVIII (1984), 189–97.

6. Other prominently cited books of the Bible were Psalms, Proverbs, Jeremiah, Chronicles, and Judges. In Deuteronomy, favorite sections included Chapters 1 (13–17), 4 (20, 23, 29–40), 5, 8, 9, 10, 27, 29, and 31. Other frequently used passages were Exodus 24 (3–8) and 25; Leviticus 24 (though all Leviticus was cited promiscuously); I Samuel 3 (11) and 20; II Samuel 7; I Kings 8 (22–66); II Kings 23 (1–3); and Joshua 4 and 5.

Table 1. Distribution of Citations

Category	1760s	1770s	1780s	1790s	1800–1805	% of Total N
Bible	24%	44%	34%	29%	38%	34%
Enlightenment	32 (21)	18 (11)	24 (23)	21 (20)	18 (17)	22 (19)
Whig	10 (21)	20 (27)	19 (20)	17 (18)	15 (16)	18 (21)
Common Law	12	4	9	14	20	11
Classical	8	11	10	11	2	9
Other	14	3	4	8	7	6
	100%	100%	100%	100%	100%	100%
	n = 216	n = 544	n = 1,306	n = 674	n = 414	N = 3,154

The categories are those developed by Bernard Bailyn (*The Ideological Origins of the American Revolution* [Cambridge, Mass., 1967]). No significant change results if we break Bailyn's Enlightenment category into the three subcategories described by D. Lundberg and H. F. May ("The Enlightened Reader in America," *American Quarterly*, XXVIII [special issue, 1976], 262–93). The First Enlightenment, dominated by Montesquieu, Locke, and Pufendorf, comprises 16 percent of all citations. The more radical writers of the Second Enlightenment, such as Voltaire, Diderot, and Helvétius, garner 2 percent. The Third Enlightenment, typified by Beccaria, Rousseau, Mably, and Raynal, receives 4 percent of the citations. The total is the 22 percent listed here for all Enlightenment writers. Bailyn's scheme is one of the most prominent, but still controversial. For example, shifting Locke to the category of Whigs, as many or most of the Founders perceived him, yields the percentages that are in parentheses.

pamphlets published during the 1770s were reprinted sermons. When reading comprehensively in the political literature of the war years, one cannot but be struck by the extent to which biblical sources used by ministers and traditional Whigs undergirded the justification for the break with Britain, the rationale for continuing the war, and the basic principles of Americans' writing their own constitutions.

References to writers identified with the European Enlightenment were fairly constant throughout the forty-five-year founding era. However, as Table 3 shows, the writers within this category changed significantly over the years. A writer's relative prominence usually varies over time. When discussing influence, we should, for example, distinguish the revolutionary years from the years surrounding the writing of the United States Constitution.

Montesquieu and Locke were most prominent during the 1760s—more than 60 percent of all references to Enlightenment thinkers. During the 1770s these two account for more than 75 percent of all Enlightenment references. It is of

Table 2. Frequency of Citation

1. Montesquieu	8.3%		19. Shakespeare	.8
2. Blackstone	7.9		20. Livy	.8
3. Locke	2.9		21. Pope	.7
4. Hume	2.7		22. Milton	.7
5. Plutarch	1.5		23. Tacitus	.6
6. Beccaria	1.5		24. Coxe	.6
7. Trenchard &			25. Plato	.5
Gordon (Cato)	1.4		26. Abbé Raynal	.5
8. De Lolme	1.4		27. Mably	.5
9. Pufendorf	1.3		28. Machiavelli	.5
10. Coke	1.3		29. Vattel	.5
11. Cicero	1.2		30. Petyt	.5
12. Hobbes	1.0		31. Voltaire	.5
13. Robertson	.9		32. Robison	.5
14. Grotius	.9		33. Sidney	.5
15. Rousseau	.9		34. Somers	.5
16. Bolingbroke	.9		35. Harrington	.5
17. Bacon	.8		36. Rapin	.5
18. Price	.8			

These thirty-six writers together account for about half of all citations. Among those just below the cut-off for this table are: Burlamaqui, Godwin, Adam Smith, Volney, Shaftesbury, Hooker, Burlingame, Hoadley, Molesworth, Priestley, Macaulay, Goldsmith, Hutcheson, Burgh, Defoe, Paley, Fortescue, Virgil, Polybius, Aristotle, and Thucydides.

Table 3. Most-Cited Secular Thinkers

	1760s	1770s	1780s	1790s	1800–1805	% of Total N
Montesquieu	8%	7%	14%	4%	1%	8.3%
Blackstone	1	3	7	11	15	7.9
Locke	11	7	1	1	1	2.9
Hume	1	1	1	6	5	2.7
Plutarch	1	3	1	2	0	1.5
Beccaria	0	1	3	0	0	1.5
Cato*	1	1	3	0	0	1.4
De Lolme	0	0	3	1	0	1.4
Pufendorf	4	0	1	0	5	1.3
Coke	5	0	1	2	4	1.3
Cicero	1	1	1	2	1	1.2
Hobbes	0	1	1	0	0	1.0
Subtotal	33%	25%	37%	29%	32%	32.4%
Others	67	75	63	71	68	67.6
	100%	100%	100%	100%	100%	100.0%
	n = 216	n = 544	n = 1,306	n = 674	n = 414	N = 3,154

The list contains more than 180 names. The last column allows more precise recovery of the number of citations over the era, but all other percentages are rounded off to the nearest whole number. The use of 0% indicates less than .5% of the citations for a given decade rather than no citations whatsoever.
* "Cato" refers to a series of pamphlets together known as *Cato's Letters,* written by the English Whigs John Trenchard and Thomas Gordon.

considerable interest that during the 1760s, references to Locke were primarily in pieces dealing with the relationship of the colonists in America to Britain. In the 1770s, references to Locke appeared most often in works justifying the break with England and the writing of new constitutions. On the other hand, writers on constitutional design cited Montesquieu heavily. As the framing of state and national constitutions continued in the 1780s, Montesquieu became so important that he alone accounts for almost 60 percent of all Enlightenment references.

Locke's rate of citation, which during the 1760s and 1770s was the highest for any secular writer, fell off drastically and did not recover. After the writing of the Constitution, references to Montesquieu also declined, and during the 1790s those authors who cited him were mainly concerned with state constitutions. This overall pattern is not at all surprising. Locke is profound on establishing a civil society and on opposing tyranny, but has relatively little to say about institutional design. Therefore he was properly influential in Americans' justifying their resistance to the Stamp Act, their break with England, and their writing their own constitutions. His influence on the *design* of any constitution, state or national, is probably exaggerated, and finding him hidden in passages of the U.S. Constitution is an exercise that requires more evidence than has hitherto been provided.

Montesquieu was prominent during the period of constitution writing, as were two other Enlightenment writers—Beccaria and De Lolme. The period of state constitution writing also brought to the fore a host of English Whig writers. Cato (Trenchard and Gordon), Hoadley, Bolingbroke, Price, Burgh, Milton, Molesworth, Priestley, Macaulay, Sidney, Somers, Harrington, and Rapin were most heavily cited during the late 1770s and through the 1780s. There were also many other Enlightenment writers cited as well, including Robertson, Grotius, Rousseau, Pope, Raynal, Mably, Burlamaqui, and Vattel. All in all, during the period of constitution writing, Enlightenment and Whig authors were cited about equally as a group, though the Whigs were nearly three times as numerous.

It is impossible to show in detail the sudden outpouring of references to these authors between 1775 and 1790. The number of citations from the 1760s to the 1770s went from 216 to 544, and then more than doubled again from the 1770s to the 1780s (544 to 1,306). Bailyn is correct that in pamphlets dealing with constitutional design, the Whig theorists were most prominent through sheer numbers. Whig and Enlightenment writers as groups were almost even between 1775 and 1790, with about twenty writers representing the latter group, and more than sixty representing the former. No Whig author even approaches Montesquieu for sheer volume or dominance of the category. Indeed, Montesquieu is almost without peer during the founding era.

Blackstone was the second most prominent secular writer, having been cited well over two and a half times as often as Locke. Whereas Locke fell from prominence after 1776, Blackstone was increasingly cited. Hume's pattern is similar. Both Blackstone and Hume are strong on governmental process and the operation and interaction of political institutions. There is a certain logic, then, in their becoming prominent when the design, operation, adjustment, and evolution of political institutions was of central concern.

Table 4 illustrates the pattern of citations surrounding the debate on the U.S. Constitution. The items from which the citations for this table are drawn come close to exhausting the literature written by both sides. Surprisingly, both sides used Enlightenment and Whig authors in about the same proportion. Montesquieu was almost twice as prominent during the debate over the national Constitution as he was for the decade as a whole, and almost three and a half times

Table 4. Citations by Federalists and Anti-Federalists, 1780s

	Federalists	Anti-Federalists	Total
Montesquieu	29%	25%	14%
Blackstone	7	9	7
Locke	0	3	1
Hume	3	1	1
Plutarch	7	0	1
Beccaria	0	4	3
Cato	2	2	3
De Lolme	0	6	3
Pufendorf	0	1	1
Coke	0	1	1
Cicero	0	1	1
Robertson	0	0	1
Lycurgus	6	1	1
Mably	7	2	2
Grotius	5	0	1
Temple	5	1	1
Price	0	2	1
Addison	0	2	.5
Vattel	0	1	.5
Sidney	1	0	.5
Subtotal	72%	62%	44.5%
Other	28	38	55.5
	100%	100%	100%
	n = 164	n = 364	n = 1,306

as prominent as he was for the entire era. Grotius and Mably were the only other Enlightenment figures mentioned prominently by the Federalists. The Anti-Federalists used De Lolme, Beccaria, Mably, Price, Vattel, and Pufendorf to their advantage. Among Whig writers, the Federalists favored Trenchard and Gordon, Temple, and Sidney, while the Anti-Federalists favored Price, Addison, and Trenchard and Gordon. Despite the differences, the most interesting finding is how similar the Federalists and Anti-Federalists were in their citation patterns. Not only do we *not* find the Federalists inclined toward Enlightenment writers and the Anti-Federalists away from them, the Federalists sometimes cited Enlightenment writers in the negative. For example, there is a lot of arguing against Montesquieu's dictum that republics must be small and homogeneous if they are to survive, while the Anti-Federalists cite Montesquieu with approval on this point.

The most frequently cited writers during the founding era were Montesquieu, Blackstone, Locke, and Hume. It is not denigrating the importance of other thinkers, either individually or collectively, to say that there appears to be some reason for paying special attention to these four. They were prominent throughout the literature of that era, in the pamphlet debate between Federalists and Anti-Federalists, and in the proceedings of the convention itself.

The last point is made with great effect by Forrest McDonald, and his analysis is most helpful in assessing the overall impact of European thinkers. McDonald notes that one of the few points upon which most delegates agreed was their seeking "to pattern the United States Constitution, as closely as circumstances would permit, after the English Constitution." [7] The problem was that the Framers were working from more than one model of the English constitution. They were in effect seeking different ends, ends that were not compatible.

One model of the English constitution was Blackstone's. He saw a mixed government wherein the Crown, Lords, and Commons were blended into a supreme Parliament. Each element was supposed to restrain the power of the others through a system of checks and balances, producing a harmonious whole. Where Blackstone saw mixture, Montesquieu saw separation. Drawing upon Bolingbroke's erroneous analysis, Montesquieu produced a model of the English constitution in which the three branches were in fact kept separate. He felt that the concentration of power in the same hands was the greatest threat to liberty. Therefore, the strength of the English constitution was that it maintained the executive, legislative, and judicial branches in such a way as to preserve liberty. Although Montesquieu was in error about Britain, his work and the pamphleteering of Thomas Paine left Americans deeply suspicious of mixed government. There were some attempts in the early state constitutions to institute something akin to separation of powers—with little success. Americans still saw that separation narrowly, as the prohibition on holding several offices at once. Otherwise, bicameralism became the major expression of separation of powers in state constitutions, and frequent elections remained the primary check upon a typically supreme legislature.

Hume provided the third model. His method was more blatantly political and based upon an analysis of factions. He saw the English constitution as characterized by two power blocs—the king and Lords versus the Commons. The Commons had control over taxation and the army, but its potential for domination was balanced by the court's prestige. In addition, the court could use pa-

7. McDonald, *Novus Ordo Seclorum,* 209.

tronage to corrupt the Commons and thus divide it internally. The vision of balanced factions held particular appeal for those Federalists who agreed with Hume that institutions were more important than virtue in the creation of good government.

In the English context these three interpretations comprised a stew of incompatible ingredients. In the American context each model had a limited relevance for their state or national constitutions. Items in the Constitution appear analogous to one model or the other, but circumstances in America were so different that it was not possible to approximate any one of the three models at the national level. On the other hand, those circumstances also made it possible to blend parts of all three. In the end, the Founders ransacked the three for ideas to use in solving American problems in a manner congruent with their own constitutional tradition.

American Circumstances

What were the circumstances in which European ideas were so transformed? First of all, American political thought in 1787 was not an empty bottle to be filled. There was a century and a half of constitutional experience. In terms of practical politics, the colonists generally elected their legislatures, and the governors were Crown-appointed. As in England, the legislature controlled the purse and had effective control of the militia. The governor, on the other hand, did not have an upper house whose members were lords since there was no aristocracy in America. For this and other reasons, attempts to divide the legislature by awarding representatives paying jobs in the executive branch failed to work. The governor faced a united legislature and had little patronage to disburse. By the middle of the eighteenth century the legislatures in most colonies had more power than did their respective governors. The colonists had evolved a form of separation of powers—holding several offices at once was generally prohibited. This undercut the patronage system, which formed the basis for Hume's analysis and which made Montesquieu's analysis less erroneous for American colonial government than it was for England's government.

Still, the adversarial mentality generated by the colonists vis-à-vis the governor did approximate Hume's power-bloc analysis. In America, though, the basis was different, and it disappeared with independence. Also, colonial government looked at first like a mixed form, but there was a gulf between the strong legislature and the executive with no aristocracy to call upon. With independence many states tried to institute a form of mixed government that would produce the harmonious blending of monarchic, aristocratic, and democratic elements in a supreme legislature. Such a government would also be congruent with the American communitarian emphasis upon homogeneity of values and rights. We earlier saw how many political essays, such as Theophilus Parsons' *Essex Result* and Adams' *Thoughts on Government,* argued explicitly for a mixed government.

Bicameralism was a popular feature of most early state constitutions as a primary means of separating the aristocratic from the democratic. Most failed in this respect since the men attracted to the upper house, despite stiffer property requirements for those who sought office there, were similar to those attracted to the lower house. The two houses thus did not differ markedly in the kinds of policies they supported. At the center of this problem lay a broad electorate, the same one that voted for both legislative branches. Plentiful land in America, among other things, had transformed England's forty-shilling voting requirement into a means of extending the broadest suffrage known to the world at that time. Geography, English common law, religion, and colonial status all conspired to create an electorate that had to elect both houses. That in turn destroyed the possibility of bicameralism as a means for instituting mixed government.

One legacy of colonial politics was a deep distrust of executives, with the result that state governors were essentially figureheads. As weak as colonial governors had been, they did have the British navy behind them, and a certain social status as well, so they could come reasonably close to limiting the legislature. The state executives after independence could not rein in the democratic element, so American constitutional government at the state level was unbalanced. Connecticut and Rhode Island were clear exceptions. By their charters, the colonists elected the governors, who had therefore been entrusted with real power. A balance closer to the mixed government model thus existed in these colonies despite the absence of an aristocracy. Again, American circumstances, primarily the experience with colonial governors who had no lords to support them, had prevented the importation of any version of English government.

Along with the colonial institutions went a theory of government with deep roots in dissenting Protestantism. The American Whig theory generated a view of politics different from that dominant in England. It also generated documents of political foundation upon which rested the written constitutions.

Sectarian diversity had significant effects. Whereas the court automatically included high officials of the Church of England, church-state relations in America were entirely different, further vitiating the utility of any model of government that had a role for the aristocracy. Perhaps even more important, sectarian diversity required the creation of institutions and practices that first expressed American pluralism. Madison's deep involvement in the issue of religious toleration, and thus his acute awareness of how to treat diversity when there was no natural majority, must have influenced his deriving by analogy a broader solution to diversity in general. Hume had a theory about dealing with factions, but Madison had direct experience. His approach to dealing with several religions may have led him to consider Hume's idea and decide it was sound.

The constitutional tradition in America had produced the expectation that any constitution could be written as a single document. All three English models relied on informal arrangements that included an aristocracy and a king. Americans' formal, written arrangements did not require any specific social structure in order to operate. That a constitution had to be written altered fundamentally the prospects for adopting English models. This simple idea transformed every aspect of politics. Ironically, it also allowed the blending of different political models.

In America, there had been several colonies, and after independence there were several states. Each had its own government that had existed for many years. No model of English government, which was unitary, could deal with these states. Their existence was one of those brute facts that rendered all English models virtually irrelevant.

The reasons why Americans did not adapt European ideas intact thus include: one hundred fifty years of colonial government; no long-entrenched, hereditary aristocracy; the world's broadest suffrage; an existing political theory; the expectation of written constitutions; religious diversity; and the existence of states with their own governments. The list could be extended, but it is long enough to illustrate that Locke, Montesquieu, Blackstone, Hume, and a hundred others gave to America ideas for a constitutional order, but America already had one. That order had to evolve to meet new circumstances, the most important of which was the sudden absence of the English Crown. The constitutional system had become unbalanced, and the Articles of Confederation was a *modus vivendi* inadequate to the circumstances.

Still, using a written constitution, the Americans did borrow from European thinkers. Montesquieu, the most widely cited, did seem to understand the process they were undergoing. He wrote of the laws' spirit conforming to the genius and circumstances of a people. Montesquieu in this regard gave voice to what Americans already believed, what they were already practicing. Americans matched their government to their circumstances because this inevitably happens in a constitutional system worthy of the name. They took Montesquieu's analysis and transformed it into an accurate prediction. They were going in that direction anyway, and brought Locke, Montesquieu, Blackstone, and Hume along with them.

12.   The Text of the Constitution

With independence, Americans faced immediately two fundamental problems of political existence. The first—how to constitute the sovereign power in place of the king—was easy. As David Ramsay said in 1789:

> The genius of the Americans, their republican habits and sentiments, naturally led them to substitute the majesty of the people, in lieu of discarded royalty. The kingly office was dropped, but in most of the subordinate departments of government, antient forms and names were retained. . . . Such a portion of power had at all times been exercised by the people and their representatives, that the change of sovereign was hardly perceptible. . . . The people felt an uninterrupted continuation of the blessings of law and government under old names, though derived from a new sovereignty, and were scarcely sensible of any change in their political constitution.

Ramsay was speaking here of state government. The second problem was more difficult—how to constitute popular sovereignty at the national level as well. Ramsay's formulation combines directness and delicacy.

> The rejection of British sovereignty not only involved a necessity of erecting independent constitutions, but of cementing the whole United States by some common bond of union. The act of independence did not hold out to the world thirteen sovereign states, but a common sovereign of the whole in their united capacity. It therefore became necessary to run the line of distinction between the local legislatures and the assembly of the states in Congress.[1]

1. David Ramsay, *The History of the American Revolution* (2 vols.; Philadelphia, 1789), I, 350, 357.

The choice of words is interesting. Independent state constitutions were erected, but the picture of a common sovereign was held out to the world. The "official" Declaration of Independence is entitled "unanimous declaration," though unanimity did not originally exist. Circumstances required America to present a united front. More problematic was how to constitute a united nation.

At first they based the national government on a compact among the states, thus reflecting popular sovereignty only indirectly. That government was too weak and dependent upon the states to be effective. In addition, state governments were not stable in the sense that they were to a degree constitutionally unbalanced. The difficulty, as Ramsay correctly perceived, was that under the Articles of Confederation, "[n]o coercive power was given to the general government, nor was it invested with any legislative power over individuals, but only over states in their corporate capacity." [2]

The obvious solution was to give the national government direct power over individuals. The problem in America was that state governments had their own constitutions, which rested on the sovereignty of their respective peoples. How could state and national governments have direct power over the same people? It was necessary, as Ramsay said, to run a line of distinction between the national and state legislatures. But how was such a line to be drawn, and how could those two legislatures be theoretically explained and justified?

The answer to the second question was more crucial. Ramsay made an important point: "The far famed social compact between the people and their rulers did not apply to the United States." [3] The reference was, of course, to John Locke. Government based upon a compact between the people and the ruler(s) was an English Whig idea, one that became unworkable on the other side of the Atlantic.

Instead, Americans had lived for more than a century and a half under two different kinds of political documents that were unknown to the English in their own country. One, typified by a charter, was a sovereign's unilateral grant that was not so much an agreement as a certification of a relationship. The sovereign had all the power in this asymmetrical arrangement. The second kind of agreement, typified by covenants and compacts, was not between a people and their rulers but among the people. In a compact and a covenant, the people agree to do something together—to form a church, to seek God's way, to form a government, to be bound by a majority in forming that government, to accept a specific kind of government. An agreement creating a people should be unanimous, for those not agreeing are not bound by it. The creation of a specific form of government, however, requires only a majority among the people created by the first

2. *Ibid.,* 357.
3. *Ibid.,* 356–57.

152 The Origins of American Constitutionalism

part of the agreement. Neither of these agreements involves the government as a party.

During the colonial era in America, the Crown unilaterally agreed to charter a colony and granted local self-government as long as its laws did not run counter to English law. Within these confines, the Americans ran local governments based upon covenants and compacts (agreements among themselves rather than with government). Under the circumstances, making an agreement between the people and government was not sensible since the government, the Crown, had already unilaterally spoken.

Furthermore, the colonists were creating legislatures, not governments in the complete sense. As Gordon S. Wood and others have noted, the colonists regarded the Crown, and the governors it appointed, as the government. The legislature represented the community to the Crown and protected the people from the government. It was not part of the government itself.[4] The legislature was thus the people assembled in miniature, and its deliberations and approval were theirs. It was therefore sensible that American legislatures wrote and adopted constitutions in the name of the people. When the people began to insist that constitutions or other kinds of legislation be returned to the people for direct approval, then the signal was that the legislature was seen as part of the government as well.

With independence a simple, straightforward, yet extraordinary logic took hold. The Crown was no longer the sovereign; the people were. The Crown did not make unilateral agreements based upon asymmetrical power; the people did. At the same time, the people continued to make agreements among themselves about what they wished to do collectively. State constitutions thus took the form of a compact in which the people agreed to pursue a specific way of life under a specific form of government, and then they unilaterally delineated the role of those in government. Such officials were viewed as agents of the people and were therefore in no position to be making compacts with the people. The colonists had practiced the *form* of popular sovereignty under the sanction of the king. After independence the American people became sovereign *in fact*, and popular sovereignty rested upon an agreement among the people.

There was therefore no inherent problem in having two legislatures, one for the state and one for the nation. The sovereign could unilaterally parcel out power as it saw fit—to different levels of government as well as to different branches at the same level of government. These were, after all, only agents getting various jobs to perform. Englishmen were subjects under the Crown, and thus their best hope was for a compact with the Crown. Americans brought

4. Gordon S. Wood, *The Creation of the American Republic, 1776–1787* (Chapel Hill, 1969), 237–38, 244–55.

with them from colonial status a sense of being citizens. Citizens were people who deliberated together on how to control their common fate. They acted rather than being acted upon. Citizens acting to create a national government were citizens of that nation. Citizens acting to create a state government were citizens of that state. Thus arose the legal fiction of dual citizenship, which, together with popular sovereignty, provided the solution to the second vexing problem following independence—how to simultaneously constitute national and state governments.

Dual citizenship built upon popular sovereignty is the fundamental premise of federalism—the delineation of the power of state and national governments. Dual citizenship is explicit in Article IV, Section 2 of the United States Constitution, and implicit in Article I, Sections 8, 9, and 10, which distribute power between the two levels of government. Dual citizenship and popular sovereignty in turn are logical extensions of the habits, institutions, and theories Americans developed during the colonial era.

Federalism lies at the heart of the United States Constitution. Without federalism, there was no practical or theoretical basis for moving much beyond the Articles of Confederation. The form of federalism had been rehearsed during the colonial years in such documents as the Fundamental Orders of Connecticut. Indeed, the concept of federalism—the creation of a new unified entity that is indissoluble yet preserves the freedom and integrity of its constituent parts—derives from the biblical notion of covenant, which the dissenting Protestant colonists understood so well.

Federalism and dual citizenship are elsewhere in the Constitution and its amendments, most prominently the Tenth and Fourteenth Amendments. Although details of the federal form remained incomplete in the Constitution, that does not detract from the importance of federalism. Details of almost every important aspect of the Constitution were left to future generations. The struggle over states' rights, judicial interpretation of the Bill of Rights as it applies to the states, and even the decline of state power versus national power operate within a framework defined by federalism. As a principle of constitutional design, federalism still exists. That Americans can still raise questions about state versus national power or about the states' modern role is one indication that they operate under the United States Constitution.

The Madisonian Model

Madison tells us that the Constitution has two goals—to preserve liberty and to create a stable, effective national government. Liberty already existed in America and did not have to be created, but preserved. Ineffectiveness at the national level had two sources: the powers granted Congress were insufficient, and

Congress could not utilize its powers to directly affect individual citizens. However, directness was a two-way street in American constitutionalism. In order for government to act directly upon the citizens, they had to be able to act directly upon it. Any constitution that solved the problem of ineffective national government would have to be approved by the citizens and would involve them in national elections. What would prevent the majority tyranny some perceived at the state level from becoming national? Expanding national powers would remove certain important matters from state majorities, such as debasing the currency to relieve debtors, but would expose these matters to national majorities and thus national tyranny. In Madison's interpretation, the solution was to expand national powers, which could act directly upon the citizens, but to so structure national government that it would have the balances lacking at the state level. Thus would the problems at both levels be solved simultaneously.

Madison begins *Federalist* 10 by noting that it is the *violence* of faction that is to be prevented, not faction itself. As we learn later, faction is part of the everyday operation of government. Further, since human nature will lead factions to resort to violence even when there is no objective tyranny, the system must somehow minimize the perception of tyranny as well as its actual existence. Madison argued that representation and the extended republic can control factions. Representation filters upward men of greater virtue, those who seek the common good rather than the partial good of any one faction. This is a traditional American Whig solution. However, Madison said, virtuous men will not always be at the helm—and even if they are, this solution will be inadequate.

Ultimately the solution lies in a republic so extended, with such a large, diverse population, that the existence of a natural majority is rendered unlikely, if not impossible. With many minority factions on a given issue, *and with the requirement for majority rule to pass policy,* any majority coalition must include several or perhaps many minorities. This will take time, the majority will be temporary, and there will be no basis for a shared passion sufficient for the majority to seek to harm the vital interests of any minority. The process of constructing a majority will create enough delay to result in policy being based upon calm calculations of interest. Minorities in the losing coalition, a temporary unity, will not be given cause for alarm over their vital interests, they will not be aroused to counter a passionate majority, and thus they will have no need to resort to violence. Hence, a stable and effective government is produced and preserved.

The Madisonian model combined the traditional Whig solution (more virtuous legislators) with a new idea, that of the extended republic. However, when we look at the Constitution to see what created the extended republic, we find the ratification requirement in Article VII and the provision in Article IV, Section 3 for admitting new states. There is nothing else in the document that is relevant to creating an *extended* republic. The two provisions that are relevant come directly from the Articles of Confederation, which the Constitution was supposed to correct. How can it be that the solution to the ineffectiveness of the Articles, the extended republic, was already in the Articles?

The answer is that commentators have overlooked the other word in *extended republic*. The nation that the Articles of Confederation created was extensive, but it was not a republic because the Continental Congress did not embody the republican principle—direct election by the people. What makes the Constitution a solution for ineffective government is that the House of Representatives in Congress will be elected by popular vote, *and thus Congress can pass laws directly affecting those who elect them*. The Articles of Confederation created an extended confederacy, but the Constitution created an extended *republic*. The key, then, is not the size of the country, but the direct involvement of a national citizenry in the government of a large country.

The extended republic was not possible without federalism, both in terms of its being extended and its being republican. First of all, Americans could not adopt a unitary government—the state governments would not disappear. They had to find a way to tie the nation together and still preserve state governments. Distributing power between the two levels of government was the answer, and this is federalism. Furthermore, the national government could not be republican in form unless its legislature was elected by the people. This, in turn, was not possible unless the government and people had a direct relationship. The creation of dual citizenship, the idea for which was implicit in the Articles of Confederation, was the answer, and this is federalism. Without federalism, there would have been no extended republic.

One can conclude that the Whigs and the Federalists both managed to get their way. From the Whig point of view, their beloved state governments were represented in the Senate. Furthermore, Article I, Section 2 of the Constitution declared the electorate for the House of Representatives to be the same as that for the lower house in the respective state legislatures. The electorate for the House would thus be defined by the states, and that same electorate would vote for the state legislatures, which would in turn elect the Senate. A few, such as Dickinson, might prefer to see the Senate as analogous to the House of Lords, and one could indeed say that it embodied the aristocratic principle as a result of the double filtering process in selecting its members. Ask the average Federalist what the Senate did, however, and he would undoubtedly answer "represent the states." The Whigs loved their states and state governments, and on balance the Senate looked to be just as much a means of satisfying Whig preferences as the House of Representatives.

The Federalists, on the other hand, felt that their goals were met. In order to understand why, we need to return to Madison's model. Having solved the

problem of majority tyranny, he turns in *Federalist* 47 through 51 to governmental tyranny, and his solution was structurally similar to that for majority
tyranny. The powers given to the national government were divided among the
two houses of the legislature and the three branches of the government. No one
part had a "majority" of the power, but the various branches must cooperate to
get the job done and at the same time must compete. Ambition effectively
counteracts ambition in a process designed to prevent all power from falling into
the same hands.

Although the solution to governmental tyranny was more complex, the net
effect was to induce delay. The Whigs had a deep love of the deliberative process,
and here the Federalists made it even more deliberative. Not much for the
Whigs to argue about in this regard.

Still, there was a subtle yet important difference in how Federalists and
Whigs thought about what constituted a virtuous people. Whigs saw that people
as seeking the common good for its own sake. Since interests were homogeneous in the long run, there was no inherent conflict between the common good
and one's long-term self-interest. Federalists, however, were inclined to see
heterogeneity of interests that could be accommodated but not made congruent, even in the long run. Nor did they see an objective common good to be
sought and discovered. They saw the possibility of the people's permanent and
aggregate interest emerging from the interaction of competing interests.

Whigs believed that a virtuous people had moral abilities and a sense of
community that led them, when necessary, to abandon self-interest for the sake
of the common good. Federalists thought that a virtuous people were able to
assess interests accurately and would then seek and reach agreements or ac-
commodations with others that advanced these interests. Out of the many ac-
commodations would come something similar to what later would be called the
greatest good for the greatest number. Both Whigs and Federalists saw a virtuous people as the basis for a system of self-government, but they defined
virtue in different ways.

Some see the institutions of delay as a means of thwarting majority will, even
of preventing majority rule. However, the entire system assumes ultimate majority rule—otherwise, the process will not work. If Madison and the others did
not intend for the majority to rule, why did they even worry about preventing
majority tyranny? Direct election of the House of Representatives, compared
with the provision in the Articles of Confederation (Congress was elected by the
state legislatures), does not look like a step away from majority rule. This and
other aspects of the U.S. Constitution argue against the elitist interpretation.

Separation of Powers, Checks and Balances, and Bicameralism

Separation of powers had its roots at least partially in the colonial attempt to
prevent the Crown-appointed governors from buying off members of the legisla-

ture. These governors, in imitation of the court in England, would offer lucrative positions in the executive branch to key members of the legislature. The colonists successfully resisted this patronage and instituted prohibitions on holding several offices at once. Most of the references to separation of powers in the early state constitutions reflect more the colonial experience than the adoption of a coherent theory. Those documents generally resembled a mixed government model.

Montesquieu was full of praise for the separation of powers in England, and his analysis, though incorrect, still deeply impressed the Americans. The United States Constitution bears the imprint of his ideas, most notably in the separate judiciary. In English practice, the judiciary was part of the executive, so the Crown was the final court of appeal. The American colonial system followed that model, but after independence the state constitutions usually put the judiciary under the legislature, which was then the final court of appeal. The idea of a separate judiciary probably came from Montesquieu. Nevertheless, contrary to his recommendation, the Supreme Court was made a permanent body with its members serving on good behavior instead of being frequently replaced.

Montesquieu gave the executive no part in legislation, aside from a veto power, and the legislature was to have no part in executing the laws, though it was to have the power of impeachment. This sounds superficially much like what exists in the United States. However, Montesquieu advised that there be two legislative bodies, the upper house representing the rich, honorable, and distinguished, the lower house representing the commoners.

As much as the Founders heeded Montesquieu and made separation of powers an important feature of the Constitution, the document in the end described more than just that. The Americans were responding to different circumstances, and they developed a different, more complex system. For one thing, in the American context the phrase "separation of powers" was a misnomer. A more accurate phrase would have been "separation of functions with shared powers." As Publius points out, if the powers were really separated, the three branches would have nothing to do with each other. In the Constitution, however, they all interlock like parts of an intricate machine. The separated functions were linked through a system of checks that resulted in shared powers.

The notion of checks was associated with the mixed form of government as described by Blackstone. In the mixed form, or mixed regime, all three functions were blended in a supreme legislature, with each function checking the others in an overall equilibrium. The English system had relatively few checks—the executive veto was prominent. By and large, the Crown used patronage to check Parliament. In the United States Constitution, there are a great number of checks. The president can veto legislation, and the legislature can override the veto with a two-thirds majority. The Senate must approve treaties made by the president, and it also approves presidential appointees. Judicial review is not in the Constitution, and thus is formally not a constitutional check. Congress can make or unmake lower courts, decide the size of the Supreme Court, determine its appellate jurisdiction, and set the salaries for the executive and judiciary. It can also impeach members of the executive and judicial branches.

In view of the checks and their implications, it is clear that the primary result of the system was the legislature's potential dominance of the other two branches. The executive had real power, unlike the executives at the state level, and the Supreme Court had a historically unprecedented level of independence. But not completely trusting a separate and independently powerful executive or judiciary, the Founders included a series of leashes, most of which led back to Congress. The executive, legislative, and judicial powers were separated to a certain degree, but then linked firmly in a partial remixing, and Congress was dominant in the mix. That is what the checks do—move the system back toward a system of mixed government. In the U.S. Constitution, however, it appears to be primarily the legislature checking the other branches—not, as Blackstone saw it, the other branches checking the legislature.

The only check that seems to fit Blackstone's model is the requirement that legislation pass an upper house as well as a lower one. In England, the House of Lords could block legislation from the House of Commons and, in league with patronage from the Crown, keep the Commons checked. In America this check worked differently. Not only were there no lords, but there were no property requirements for senatorial candidates. The Senate does in a sense check the House, but the reverse is also true. Furthermore, most of the Senate's explicit checks are aimed not at the House but at the executive. A better way to understand the United States Senate, rather than through European theory, is through the colonial political experience.

During the colonial era, legislatures were unicameral with no real upper house, and a privy council (composed of the "better sort") was supposed to "advise" the governor. The governors hoped thereby to separate the more powerful and wealthy men and use them as an instrument for furthering the Crown's ends. Unfortunately for the governors, the privy councils tended to overadvise the governors, and their advice invariably matched the legislators' suggestions. In effect, the privy council came to be a means for the people or their legislators to check the executive rather than a means for the executive to check the legislature. After independence, all but two states created a bicameral legislature. One purpose of the upper house was to make the legislative process more deliberative, but another purpose was to keep a close eye on the executive. In many state constitutions the executive could not act unless he had the concurrence of a committee or council drawn from the legislature, usually from the upper house. The United States Senate seems to fit this mold. It is a sort of check on the House because both houses must pass every bill. Primarily, however, the Senate seems oriented toward the executive as a means of keeping track of him.

Even having the vice-president preside in the Senate can be read this way. Voting only in case of a tie, and not being part of the deliberations, he must nonetheless listen to what the Senate has to say about the executive branch. It is an excellent forum: senators can send a message to the president without having that prestigious person there to affect the discussion. If the vice-president later becomes president, the Senate has effectively educated him rather directly about the Senate's point of view. Still, having the vice-president preside in the Senate, and giving him a vote in evenly balanced and therefore probably politically sensitive matters, do provide a check by the executive upon the Senate. Although most checks enhance control by the legislature, they also link the three branches and thus undercut the separation of powers.

In addition, the mixing of powers is furthered by the Supreme Court's part in the impeachment of the president, and by the impeachment process itself. Contrary to what some commentators have to say, there is little evidence that the impeachment power was anything but a political tool. Congress could impeach a president or a member of the Supreme Court who failed to meet political criteria, not just those who committed crimes. Thus, by implication, the legislature was involved in the execution and the adjudication of laws. Congress historically was reluctant to use impeachment for this purpose, and the current institution of impeachment has evolved through historical practice rather than formal constitutional amendment. Even someone who feels that impeachment was intended for use only in instances of criminal behavior will have to admit that Congress thus participates in a judicial proceeding, even if only removing the person from office.

The political system that the Constitution established is rather strange by European standards. Initially it seems to be a document about separation of powers, but the functions are separated, not the powers. Another quick glance shows a mixed government with the branches in balance. Further analysis reveals, however, that the legislature has a preponderance of checks so it can keep a rein on the other branches. The checks that are supposed to balance are here used to unbalance the powers and mix them. The resulting political system resembles a hopeless (by European standards) mélange of the separation of powers and the mixed government models. The United States Constitution seems most like an evolved version of state governments.

Hume's analysis of the English constitution also suffered in translation to the American context. There was no royal court of aristocrats to form a faction against the House of Commons. American colonial politics did have a split between the governor and the legislature, but factionalism did not progress as Hume described. Hume's contribution to American constitutionalism lies in his suggesting two important methodological principles. The first was the admonition to analyze politics in terms of factions rather than in terms of principles such as separation of powers. His analysis of the factional alignments in England likely had no relevance in America, but his method of analysis did. The second was his insistent preference for hemming in human nature through clearly delineated institutions rather than relying upon the development or identification of virtuous men.

England's written constitution comprised all acts of Parliament, decisions by the courts, and proper acts of the Crown. What Hume therefore meant by "wise regulations" was more on the order of administrative procedures, like those worked out for the courtroom. He says, "In the smallest court or office, the stated forms and methods, by which business must be conducted, are found to be a considerable check on the natural depravity of mankind." [5] Hume was not dealing with constitutional design; he was speaking of a formal set of regular rules, known to the public, to ensure that everyone was treated fairly. Today we might call such rules "bureaucratic procedures." Each office was to have procedures so that its operation would remain fair and predictable.

The Federalists as a group were more pessimistic about human nature than were the Whigs, and they were more willing to admit that self-interest was to be expected and was legitimate. They did not, however, see a need for a Leviathan, as did Hobbes, or for endless finely tuned regulations surrounding each governmental office. Closer to their perspective was Adam Smith's view that self-interest had redemptive qualities, so it was benign in the long run and, when properly channeled, a major force for achieving human good. It is probable that Madison *et al.* read Hume as saying roughly the same.

More important, when Americans read Hume they thought not of many small regulations hemming in each political office but of broader procedural descriptions in a written constitution. Once again the facts of American circumstances and experience altered the way in which a European's ideas were appropriated. We can see Hume's influence on the U.S. Constitution as twofold. First, Madison and Hamilton, especially in *Federalist* 10, used a critical part of Hume's theory without attribution.[6] Less obviously, the style and content of the Constitution reflect Americans' attention to Hume's admonition to emphasize

5. Thomas Hill Greene and Thomas Hodge Grose (eds.), *Hume's Philosophical Works* (4 vols.; London, 1886), III, 105–106.

6. Douglas Adair first made this connection in his famous "'That Politics May Be Reduced To A Science': David Hume, James Madison, and the Tenth *Federalist*," *Huntington Library Quarterly*, XX (1957), 343–60.

institutions rather than manners and custom. This becomes more obvious when we compare the text of the national Constitution with the texts of the state constitutions.

For example, there is a tendency to use hortatory techniques:

> The legislative, executive, and judiciary department, shall be separate and distinct, so that neither exercise the powers properly belonging to the other: nor shall any person exercise the powers of more than any one of them, at the same time; except that the Justices of the County Courts shall be eligible to either House of Assembly. (Virginia Constitution, 1776)

> In the government of this commonwealth, the legislative department shall never exercise the executive and judicial powers, or either of them: the executive shall never exercise the legislative and judicial powers, or either of them: the judicial shall never exercise the legislative and executive powers, or either of them: to the end it may be a government of laws and not of men. (Part the First, Section XXX, Massachusetts Constitution, 1780)[7]

Virtually every state constitution written between 1776 and 1787 prohibited holding several offices at once. Only these two passages seem to generalize toward a broader notion of separation of powers. Despite these clear admonitions, Virginia had the legislature elect the governor and the court, and the governor was a virtual political prisoner to a "Council of State," which the legislature elected from its own ranks. Massachusetts did better: its executive and legislative branches were in effect separated, and the relationship between them was close to that delineated in the national Constitution. However, the United States Constitution eschews any admonitory statement of principle and instead establishes separation of powers through the combined impact of the first sentence in each of the first three articles:

> All legislative Powers herein granted shall be vested in a Congress of the United States, which shall consist of a Senate and House of Representatives . . .
> The executive Power shall be vested in a President of the United States of America . . .
> The judicial Power of the United States, shall be vested in one supreme Court, and in such inferior Courts as the Congress may from time to time ordain and establish.

7. Francis N. Thorpe (ed.), *The Federal and State Constitutions, Colonial Charters, and Other Organic Laws of the United States* (7 vols.; Washington, D.C., 1907), VII, 3815, III, 1893.

The organizing principles of the Constitution are never mentioned by name. Instead, they are embodied in simple descriptions of the institutions and how they are to operate.

The U.S. Constitution is not especially long. The institutions and procedures described are so designed that there is no need for great detail. Almost any possibility falls into one of the institutions and/or procedures. The great simplifying factor is the existence of state constitutions. With a straightforward and limited grant of power to the national government, many of the complicated matters, such as the police power, education, and local government, are left at the state level.

Of particular interest in this regard, Article I, Section 2 defined the electorate for the House of Representatives as identical to that for each state's lower house, leaving to the states the definition of voters for national representatives. The Senate was elected by the state legislatures, and their respective electorates were determined by state law. The president was elected by an electoral college, and originally each state legislature decided how to designate such electors. For men supposedly worried about the operation of state governments, Federalists put an unusual amount of trust in them.

In effect, the qualifications (beyond age and residency), nomination, and election of all federal officers except the Supreme Court were outside the control of the national government, and explicitly under the control of state governments. According to Article I, Section 4 of the Constitution, Congress would regulate the time, place, and manner of elections but not the qualifications for voting and the nomination process. Even the congressional districts would be drawn by the respective state legislatures, though Congress could determine apportionment as long as each state had one seat and the number of seats was proportional to the population recorded in a census taken every ten years. The Founders seem to be telling us that some things about elections were not crucial to the operation of the Constitution, such as the characteristics of voters and of those who run for office. What was important with regard to elections? The strange answer is, the size and nature of constituencies, the frequency of elections, and the size of the two houses of Congress.

In discussions of the Constitution, the standard practice is to run "checks" together with "balances" almost as if they are one word. They are not the same, or even similar. Nor does *balance* refer to balances within the national government—between the two houses, for example, or between the president and Congress. The term has little to do with the sense of scales and equilibrium. Rather, it refers to a mechanism or mechanisms for regulating the speed at which something occurs. This definition resembles the one used during the eighteenth century by clockmakers, or by physicists such as Isaac Newton. In pointing out the balances in the Constitution, we finish the Madisonian model.

The first significant balance is the different terms of office for the major institutions. Let us suppose that a faction is attempting to gain control of the national government and manages to inflame a good portion of the electorate into joining them. First they must gain a majority in the House of Representatives. Perhaps they do win in the next election, but only one-third of the Senate was up for reelection. So they must wait two more years to gain control of the Senate. They also must wait until then to win the presidency. Otherwise, a president can veto the legislation, and with only one-third of the Senate instead of the required two-thirds majority, the veto cannot be overridden. Here is one example of how the checks come into play to support the balances. Then there is the Supreme Court, which would fight a rearguard action against desired changes in public policy. The justices would have to die off to be replaced, be impeached, or be cowed by public opinion. The different terms of office mean that a faction must put together a majority and keep it together for at least four years, probably longer.

The second major balance results from the different constituencies to which each part of the government is beholden. Each member of the House has a relatively small constituent group that is mostly concerned with local issues. Any faction attempting to gain control of the House must either find an issue that attracts most congressional districts, an unlikely event in an extended republic, or else find a way to link the issue to local concerns. Then the faction must win over a majority of state legislatures to gain control of the Senate (as it was in the Constitution originally). State legislators are likely to be harder to fool or convince than the average voter, and it would take a different kind of politicking. Also, these legislators have state interests that must be addressed. Then the faction would have to persuade a majority in the electoral college to vote for its presidential candidate. The constituency for the Supreme Court is the president and the Senate. Each constituency has different characteristics and requires a different kind of approach and more careful argumentation. If a faction, after four or more years, manages to gain control of the two houses of Congress and the presidency, then it deserves to get its legislation. It is the kind of majority that should be in power.

The two balances interact with each other, the extended republic, and federalism to produce an interlocking effect. It resembles nothing so much as the workings of a clock or some other machine with gears, levers, and springs. At no point does the model assume that virtuous men will prevent majority tyranny. The assumption is that everyone following his own interest will result in a highly deliberative (*i.e.,* slow) process. Legislators are assumed to do what a majority of their respective constituents tell them to do. There is no Mr. Smith going to Washington to hurl himself before the juggernaut of injustice.

We see how the various parts of the Constitution work together to produce a coherent effect. The effect is not antimajoritarian. In fact, we can see now why the checks generally run in favor of Congress. The president and the Supreme Court are the easiest branches to capture through covert politics. Majority will is expressed most directly through Congress, and those in control can rein in either or both of the other branches if they get too far out of line. In the long run, majorities composed of those whose permanent, aggregate interests are threatened will remain intense long enough to gain control of the government. These majorities ought to win.

The balances affect not only the speed of the deliberative process, they also help structure the political process in Congress. Toward this end the size of the two bodies was also relevant and linked to the balances. Madison discussed in *The Federalist* the proper size of a legislature. According to what Vincent Ostrom calls Madison's "size principle," a legislature that is too small runs the risk of being dominated by a strong personality or a small cabal. A legislature that is too large cannot communicate effectively internally and is unable to deliberate or get anything done until, inevitably, it comes under the domination of a small organized cadre that destroys its deliberative function through strict internal control.[8]

What, then, is a good size for a deliberative body? The Constitution and Madison's notes and essays give us only hints. The Constitution has the strange provision in Article I, Section 2 that "[t]he number of Representatives shall not exceed one for every thirty Thousand [inhabitants]." This apparently means one representative for every thirty thousand people, but in fact each representative must have *at least* thirty thousand inhabitants in his district. This provision effectively prevents the House from being too large, at least at first. The rest of the passage apportions a number of representatives to each state. The total for all states is sixty-five. Madison says in *The Federalist* that five thousand is not a better number than five hundred, and that the problems of size are present in a legislature of two hundred.

The new Senate had twenty-six members, so that was not too small a number. If it were, the Founders could have apportioned three senators per state to increase the total to thirty-nine. One senator per state would have made the election of one-third every two years more difficult to organize, but would probably have been too small. Article I, Section 2 seems to imply rather clearly that the number of inhabitants per representative can be expected to increase in the future—thirty thousand is a minimum, not an optimal number. If it is assumed that the American population would continue to grow, a constituency would have to grow or the House would become too large. It is probable that the

8. Vincent Ostrom, *The Political Theory of a Compound Republic: Designing the American Experiment* (2nd ed.; Lincoln, Nebr., 1987), 92–101.

decision by Congress to increase the number of seats had that result. Just as a working approximation, the House became too large by the standards of Madison's size principle sometime around the 1860s when the members (over two hundred) moved to specialized committees. By the time the House froze its size at four hundred thirty-five members, the size principle had been violated.

Regardless, the Founders felt that size would affect the character of deliberations, as would the constituencies to which members were beholden. The House was expected to be more localist in its orientation; the Senate would be responsive to the states' more general, aggregate perspective. The senators were more likely to be calm, confident, and independent, as was usually true of successful men of some means, while the representatives might be rawer and less polished, but also more energetic and closer in perspective to the population in general. Thus, using Hume's institution-oriented approach, the Founders used the balances and the size principle to structure the kinds of deliberations that would take place. They were dealing not with the virtues of people but with human beings' natural proclivities.

A final word about the Madisonian model is in order. The Federalists derived from Hume not only a propensity for relying upon human nature channeled by institutions. They also worked from a scientific perspective to which Hume and Montesquieu were only two of many contributors. When reading *The Federalist* and other writings from the founding era, one cannot but be struck by the appearance of three widely held assumptions: that there is order in the universe; that we can know that order through observation and reason; and that we can use that natural order in constructing our political institutions. Even ministers reflected these assumptions in their sermons and were not loath to cite Newton and Locke as well as James and John. The divine law based upon revelation and the laws of nature derived from reason and science were seen at this time to be different reflections of God's mind, and thus in harmony.

The connection between the natural sciences and the "science of politics" (as it is called in *The Federalist*) was a commonplace in political discourse during the entire founding era. For example, a striking exchange took place between John Dickinson and James Wilson at the convention on June 7, 1787.

> Let our Government be like that of the Solar system; let the General Government be the Sun and the States the Planets repelled yet attracted, and the whole moving regularly and harmoniously in their respective Orbits. [Part of an extended comment by Dickinson]

> He was not, however, for extinguishing these planets as was supposed by Mr. Dickinson. Neither did he on the other hand believe that they would warm or enlighten the Sun. Within their proper orbits they must still be suffered to act for subordinate purposes for which their existence is made

essential by the great extent of country. [Madison's notes on lengthy comments by James Wilson]

Experience has evinced a constant tendency in the states to encroach on the federal authority. . . . A negative was the mildest expedient that could be devised for preventing these mischiefs. . . . This prerogative of the General Government is the greatest pervading principle that must control the centrifugal tendencies of the States; which without it, will continually fly out of their proper orbits and destroy the order and harmony of the political system. [Madison's comments in part][9]

The Federalist is replete with Newtonian terminology that Montesquieu and especially Hume helped transmit. Often it is used metaphorically, but more frequently words such as tendency, revolution, balance, equilibrium, fulcrum, system, reaction, mass, power, and many others are used with a physical scientist's precision and intent.

Blackstone's legal language, Locke's political terminology, and the scientific terms found in Montesquieu and Hume all informed American political discourse and helped shape the contents of the Constitution. But in the end, the Europeans' language, ideas, and models were fit into preexisting frames of influence from the American constitutional tradition and American experience. These earlier frames were bent, more lushly filled, and built upon, but never broken or rejected. The origins of the American Constitution, like the constitutional tradition of which it is a part, are complex and manifold, but ultimately planted firmly in American soil.

9. Max Farrand (ed.), *The Records of the Federal Convention of 1787* (4 vols.; New Haven, 1966), I, 153 (Dickinson and Wilson), 164 (Madison).

Conclusion: An Unfinished Constitutional Tradition

Over the past few years the following passage from *The Federalist* has been quoted enough times, so that it approaches the status of cliché:

> It has been frequently remarked, that it seems to have been reserved for the people of this country by their conduct and example, to decide the important question, whether societies of men are really capable or not, of establishing good government from reflection and choice, or whether they are forever destined to depend, for their political constitutions, on accident and force.[1]

Still, the passage has power and precision deserving of a wide familiarity, and it is also relevant here. After an examination of the documents defining the American constitutional tradition, it is difficult not to agree with Hamilton that the American political system is an experiment in government directed by a free people using reflection and choice as opposed to accident or force, an experiment whose ultimate outcome must remain always in doubt. We could also call upon Thomas Jefferson, who said that each generation must leave its page in America's unfolding story, and that that ability was part of the story's historical significance. At the same time, neither man believed that the experiment proceeded without rules for distinguishing a valid from an invalid outcome, or that any generation could with impunity start a completely new story, change the major outline of the plot, or disown earlier chapters. There is an underlying set of commitments that define not only the proper methodology of the experiment but also the criteria for its failure. These commitments permit continuing updates and also limit what can be considered valid extensions of the story as opposed to the ultimate rejection of its meaning or else a descent into gibberish.

1. Alexander Hamilton, James Madison, and John Jay, *The Federalist,* ed. Jacob E. Cooke (Cleveland, 1967), 3.

An honest examination of the origins of American constitutionalism thus leaves us in an interesting yet uncomfortable position when it comes to assessing the intentions of the Founders. We are unable to say with certainty who the Founders were. "The Founders" usually refers to those at the Constitutional Convention, a standard practice that is at variance with the facts. Certainly those who attended the ratifying conventions must be considered among the Founders, as were those Whigs who wrote the state constitutions that are part of the complete text of the United States Constitution. Without the contents of those earlier documents, just as would have been the case without ratification, there would have been no Constitution.

But what of those who wrote and signed the Declaration of Independence? Since the Declaration is also part of the Americans' foundation compact, as is the Articles of Confederation, then their authors belong among the Founders. The ratifying conventions were also responsible, along with the Anti-Federalist opposition in general, for the addition of the Bill of Rights, which was written by the first United States Congress and adopted by another round of state conventions. But the Judiciary Act of 1789 completed a part of the political system left undone in the Constitution, as did Chief Justice Marshall's machinations in *Marbury* v. *Madison* (1803).

If it is reasonable to speak of a founding era that lasted from about 1765 to 1805, during which the theory and institutions informing the state and national constitutions took definite form, it is also reasonable to see the era of constitution writing from 1776 to 1787 as resting firmly upon developments in America that began in 1620. In sum, there is no reason to conclude that in a given year giants in American political thought bequeathed THE WORD, which Americans must obey regardless of their experiences, commitments, needs, or circumstances. Just as American constitutionalism developed continually from 1620 to 1789 on the basis of American circumstances and commitments, it has continued to do so since 1789. The commitments remain essentially the same, though changing circumstances have required constitutional evolution. Equally important, those who wrote the United States Constitution required that citizens complete the project.

Earlier it was said that the United States Constitution was an incomplete text without the state constitutions, but it is still incomplete even with them. At the very least, "the founding" did not accomplish the union into one people. The Bicentennial did not celebrate a founding that was over and done with by a certain date. Rather, Americans celebrated those underlying commitments found in their national compact written during the founding era, commitments that were developed long before 1776 and that continue to define America today, but whose implications are still not completely resolved.

The most important commitment was to live together as a people, but as of 1789 there was no settled basis for determining who was to be included among the people and no developed sense of what inclusion meant or entailed. There were aspirations for nationhood, but they required a commonly held set of virtues not always viewed as part of the moral possessions of many who were in fact residing in America.

During the early colonial era, the Bible answered many of these questions, the relative homogeneity of the population eased the problems further, and the availability of unsettled land meant that those under suspicion of lacking sufficient virtue had somewhere to go. Moving westward became the ultimate solution to these questions. The Bible's decline as the center of American culture, increasing heterogeneity, and the closing of the frontier did not invalidate the commitment to live together but made it more problematic.

The story of American constitutionalism since 1789 is the story of a move toward a more perfect union. The Founders would never have expected Americans to create a perfect union, nor should the citizens, but the commitment is to work at making it better. The status of slaves, the situation of the native American, the controversies over illegal aliens, the civil rights movement, the New Deal, the renewed interest in the role of religion in politics, the protest movements of the 1960s, the women's movement—all these political phenomena and more are Americans' continuing contribution to the extended deliberation on the questions of who is to be included among the people, what being included means, what kinds of activities, responsibilities, rights, or liberties are thereby entailed, what virtues are requisite for a political system that rests ultimately upon the virtues of the people, and how to encourage or produce these virtues.

In recent years a debate has raged over whether and to what extent the Supreme Court should be guided by the intentions of the Founders. One consequence of this analysis of American constitutionalism is that the question generating the controversy is badly put. The Supreme Court is limited to only a part of the national compact, and thus to only a part of the intentions of the Founders. They are hamstrung in determining those intentions to the extent they cannot bring the full foundation compact to bear. Nor is it clear that even then the Supreme Court is the only political body that should concern itself with the intentions of the Founders.

The justice who said that the Constitution is whatever the Supreme Court says it is got it exactly wrong. He forgot about the rest of the country. He and his colleagues have been put in an untenable position. Instead of amending the Constitution using the process laid out therein, or the legislative process also outlined there, Americans have made a false turn in leaving it up to a non-majoritarian, legalistic process that cannot even bring the full founding agreement to bear. The Supreme Court may be the conscience of America, but ultimately whether that conscience is correct or not is up to a majority, using the political process in the Constitution, to decide.

In the meantime, the Supreme Court is asked to decide important cases bearing upon how Americans as members of a people relate to each other. The justices must find in their partial document a basis for preserving continuing American commitments—there are no pat answers in the Constitution. Not only is the Court using part of what contains the Founders' intentions, the political process since 1789 has changed, as has the reading of those words as Americans have gone about completing their foundation as a people.

It is a mistake to suppose that that is a job solely or primarily for the Supreme Court. The Court helps the citizenry avoid the mistakes a majority can sometimes make, but ultimately the operation of the entire political system as defined by the Constitution is designed to prevent majority tyranny. Let the Court do its job as well as it can, and let the rest of the citizens do theirs, in part by using the political system and not leaving it to the Court to complete the Americans' founding as a people.

This book is a small part of the attempt during the Bicentennial to help the Founders speak to Americans of their hopes and aspirations, their convictions and commitments, so that Americans can speak more clearly to each other as members of a wildly diverse, liberty-loving, self-defining, self-governing *people*.

Index